Jersey

Sonia Hillsdon

The Author

Sonia Hillsdon is a writer and local historian who has now lived in Jersey for many years. Her time working for various Island publications has necessitated a great deal of research into Jersey's past, whilst her enthusiasm for cycling and walking has enabled her to explore the Jersey of today. She is, therefore, well able to share all those details, both factual and fascinating, that will help visitors make the most of their stay in the island. Mrs Hillsdon is a member of La Société Jersiaise and the author of *Jersey Witches, Ghosts and Traditions*, *Jersey Occupation Remembered*, *Strange Stories from Jersey* (fiction), *A Taste of Jersey* and *The Jersey Lily* (Lillie Langtry) as well as a series of illustrated local history books for children including *Gorey Castle* and *Strange Goings-on in the Parishes*.

Author's Note

Different spellings and the choice, in some instances, of either French or English for Island place names on maps and signposts and in written material only serve to illustrate the bilingualism of Jersey and the influence of both Normandy and England on the island.

Dedication

In loving and grateful memory of my husband Monty Doong.

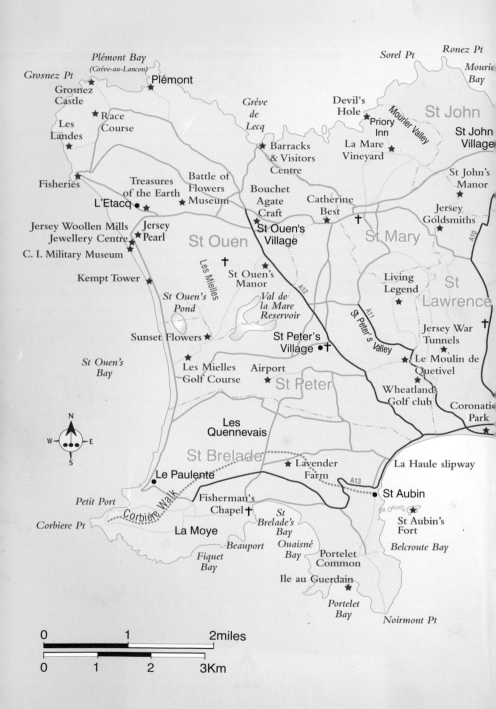

Jersey

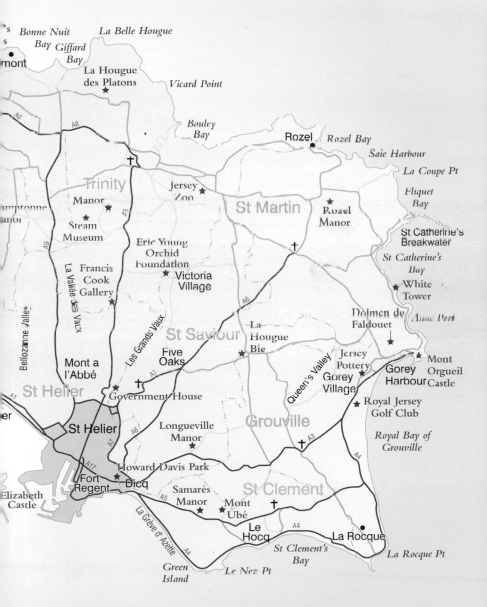

Contents

Welcome to
Jersey

Jersey – a small island in the English Channel which has given its name to a jumper, a breed of cows, a potato, a lily and even an American state! The French writer Victor Hugo considered it 'un ravissant pays'; the English novelist George Eliot delighted in its 'glimpses of the sea at unexpected openings'. Between the wars, in the 1920s and 30s, young UK couples chose Jersey as their 'honeymoon island'. Today, Jersey remains a unique and enchanting place, with its delightful mixture of traditional and modern, and a character all of its own.

Opposite page: Corbière lighthouse.

Left: Kempt Tower, the largest Jersey Tower.

Top Tips

Elizabeth Castle (page 23–25) sixteenth-century castle, spectacularly situated in St Aubin's Bay.

Hamptonne (page 117–18)
Manor House and traditional farm with animals, nature trail and restaurant offering island dishes.

Jersey Museum (page 44)
Jersey"s premier museum, with an excellent Brasserie, situated in St Helier.

Jersey Pottery (page 77)
Local Pottery, restaurant, museum, Glaze Craze paint it yourself' studio.

Jersey Zoo (page 101)
World famous Zoo, headquarters of the Durrell Wildlife Conservation Trust.

La Hougue Bie (page 69)
A massive prehistoric mound, museum and shop on site.

La Mare Vineyard (page 133)
A fine eighteenth - century house and working vinery: follow the Vineyard Trail, wine-tasting, buy from the Vineyard shop.

Living Legend (page 161)
Lots to do for the kids including adventure golf, go-karting and award winning special effects shows.

Maritime Museum & Occupation Gallery (page 44)
Nautical exhibits and the Occupation tapestry depicting life on the island under German Occupation are displayed.

Mont Orgueil Castle (Gorey Castle) (page 84)
An impressive castle overlooking Gorey harbour, great views.

Orchid Foundation (page 103-104)
Staggering displays of orchids growing in hot-houses.

Pallot's Steam, Motor & General Museum (page 98)
A large transport collection on display.

Highlights (in no particular order)

Great beaches/beach sports; Lots of sunshine; Cheap car hire; No VAT; Jersey Cream; No language barrier; Minutes away by air (Go Green – Go Jersey)

Part of Jersey's charm for the million or so visitors it attracts each year is its special blend of things French and British. Many roads have French names – La Grande Route de St Martin, Rouge Bouillon, Le Mont Sohier, La Rue des Landes – but traffic still drives on the left. In the shopping centres, near branches of well-known British stores, stand the Jersey shops of Voisin and De Gruchy, yet the assistants speak English and the currency is sterling. Visitors can feel abroad one minute, sampling *fruits de la mer* at a pavement café, or quite at home the next, enjoying a Jersey cream tea in one of the island's colourful gardens.

This dual flavour comes from Jersey's history but also, in part, from its geographical position. The largest and most southerly of the Channel Islands, it lies in the Bay of Mont-St-Michel, only about 30 miles from the Breton port of St Malo. From its northern cliffs not only can the other Channel Islands of Guernsey, Herm, Sark and Alderney be seen but also, to the east, the long stretch of the Normandy coast – at its closest only 14 miles (22.5km) across the water. The south coast of England, on the other hand, is nearly 100 (161km) miles away to the north.

The island itself measures only 9 miles (14.5km) by 5(8km) or, in the traditional Jersey measurement, covers about 65,000 *vergées*, so nowhere is more than 2½ miles (4km) from the sea. It owes its favourable climate and sunshine records both to the presence of the Gulf Stream and to the fact that the land slopes from its precipitous cliffs in the north to sea level in the south.

Its 50 miles (80.5km)of coastline, including 20 miles (32.25km) of sandy beaches, is not only extremely varied but is also subject, at full moon and at the equinox, to unusually low and high tides. The network of caves and sheltered coves on the north coast results from the erosive action of the sea over the centuries on the island's predominantly granite rocks, whose warm, pinky tones feature in so much of Jersey's architecture.

Jersey's History

Traces of Jersey's prehistory still exist today. From the time when the island was part of the continent, there are remnants of a great French forest. These black stumps of trees, when there is an exceptionally low tide, can be seen sticking through the sand at St Ouen. Flints and crude stone tools were left by hunters in La Cotte à la Chèvre (Goat's Cave) – now perched 60ft (18m) above the present level of the sea on the north coast of St Ouen – and in La Cotte de St Brelade, one of the most important Palaeolithic sites in Europe. The impressive stone monuments which have overlooked the sea round the island since Neolithic times were an integral part of the burial rites and religious ceremonies of Jersey's first farmers for over a thousand years.

If the Romans ever came to Jersey, nothing substantial remains of their time here, though there is a building at the base of the huge Pinnacle Rock in St Ouen which some suggest was a Roman-Celtic shrine to a local deity.

One of the earliest holy places to which Christian pilgrims came was the rocky outcrop, south of where Elizabeth Castle now stands, on which the hermit and martyr St Helier lived and preached to the islanders in the sixth-century. Six hundred years later the oratory, known today as the Hermitage, was built on the rock to honour the saint.

It was probably Saxon pirates who murdered St Helier on the beach of the town which now bears his name, but it is certainly to the later Viking pirates that Jersey owes its longstanding French connection. All during the ninth century these marauders from the north, or Normans as they were called, came in the summer months to plunder the Channel Islands *en route* to and from their coastal raids on England and France. They even sailed up the River Seine to besiege Paris.

This was when the French king, Charles the Simple, realised that to stop the pirate chief Rollo and his followers from terrorising his subjects, his only recourse was to bargain with him. In the treaty of 911, Rollo agreed to keep the peace in exchange for the region around Rouen which today is known as Normandy – the land of the Normans. Thus was forged an important link in Jersey's connection with France, for Rollo's son William, when he became Duke of Normandy, incorporated the Channel Islands into the duchy. So from 933 to 1204 Jersey was ruled from Normandy.

The results of these centuries of direct French rule can still be seen in the Jersey of today. Jersey men and women who claim Norman ancestry often share with their Norman counterparts the same traits of self-reliance, industry, reticence and thrift. The so-called local 'patois' some Jersey families still speak among themselves is correctly known as Jersey Norman-French; their granite houses are reminiscent in their architecture of the farmhouses in Normandy.

That the island is divided into fiefs, as well as into twelve parishes each with its church, and that several fiefs still have their manor house – some with their Seigneur, or Lord of the Manor – also harks back to the days of Norman feudal rule. Many Jersey laws, too, go back to that time, being based on Le Grand Coutumier de Normandie, and are written in French.

One such law is the right to raise La Clameur de Haro. This is done when an islander wishes to stop someone from harming his property. He falls down on his knees in the presence of two witnesses and calls out 'Haro! Haro! Haro! *à l'aide mon prince, on me fait tort.*' (Haro! Haro! Haro! to my aid, my prince, I am being wronged.) Nothing further may be done to his property until the case has been heard in a court of law. Some believe that the word 'Haro' is a direct appeal to Rollo or Rou, the first Duke of Normandy.

The Dukes of Normandy, including William the Conqueror and his descendants who were also Kings of England, continued to rule Jersey and the other Channel Islands from Rouen until war broke out, at the beginning of the thirteenth-century, between King John and France. In this war, King John lost all his French possessions, including Normandy. So, in 1204, when they were given the choice, Channel Islanders elected to owe their allegiance to the English throne and break their ancient tie with France. Centuries later, an English monarch who had good cause to be grateful to the continued loyalty of his Jersey subjects was Charles II. During the English Civil War, knowing himself to be safe from Parliament's troops, he twice took refuge in Elizabeth Castle, first as Prince of Wales and then as the proclaimed but still exiled King of England.

This change in allegiance, however, put Jersey in a vulnerable position for the perpetual hostilities between England and France continued right up to the nineteenth-century. Not only was the island in danger because of its own proximity to the French mainland, but also as the first line of defence against a French invasion of England. So fortifications against the French can be seen all round the island. Mont Orgueil Castle, by the order of King John himself, was built in the thirteenth-century to guard the approaches to the island's east coast; Elizabeth Castle, named after Elizabeth I, was started in the sixteenth-century to defend the growing town of St Helier. The various towers round the coast were

part of the defence against a much-feared French invasion between 1778 and the Napoleonic Wars.

These defences were, however, penetrated by the French on several occasions. In 1461 French troops seized, through the treachery of a Jersey man, Mont Orgueil Castle itself and from it ruled the island with great severity for seven years. In 1781 an expedition, led by the French adventurer, de Rullecourt, landed at La Rocque one January night and marched as far as the Royal Square without a shot being fired against them. It was only the bravery of Major Peirson, an officer of the English garrison stationed in Jersey at the time, that prevented a further French occupation.

The most modern fortifications to be seen all over the island are German. They date back to World War II when the only part of Great Britain to be occupied by the Nazis was the Channel

(Continued on page 16)

Walking on the north coast.

Noirmont Battery.

Grève de Lecq barracks.

Beaches

There are many to choose from and some beaches are more suitable for certain activities than others, for example St Ouens is recommended for building sandcastles, hunting for beach worms and generally running around; La Corbière for rockpooling and netting shrimps and crabs. Scallop shells can be collected in the shadow of Mont Orgueil and it is also a vast play area at low tide.

The north coast has many unexpected coves and more excellent rock pools.

For the older and more adventurous, the sport of BloKarting is available: one can zoom across St Ouen's Sand at the helm of a 3-wheeled buggy powered by a miniature sail. Sea-kayaking and kite surfing are also fun and exhilarating but not for the faint hearted! Bouley Bay on the north coast is one of the best places for scuba-diving, there is even an underwater 'Nature Trail' map available (Bouley Bay Diving Centre).

Beach festivals include 'Wet & Wild Week' and 'Beach Iron Man', also moon-walking and guided walks across the sands through hollows and rock pools.

Indoor Watersports are to be found at Aqua Splash, part of the Waterfront Centre at St Helier, and family fun swimming at Les Quennevais Sports Centre. Addresses in Factfile: see page 180-2

Beaches

North	South	West
Bonne Nuit Bay	Beauport	St Ouen's Bay
Bouley Bay	Green Island	
Grève de Lecq	La Rocque	
Plémont	Le Hocq	
East	Ouaisné Bay	
Anne Port	Portelet Bay	
Archirondel	St Aubin's Bay	
Royal Bay of Grouville	St Brelade's Bay	

For details of Adventure Companies and Sports Centres etc see FactFile

Parking at all the beaches shown on the map

W/C at all the beaches except Portelet (w/c at café for patrons)

Beach Guard at Grève de Lecq, Plémont, St Brelade's and St Ouen's (swim between yellow flags, do not swim when red flag flies)

Watch tidal flow at St Clements Bay; steps at Beauport; Plémont (lots); St Ouen's Bay (but ramp at south end)

Refreshments at all except Anne Port, Beauport, La Rocque (Portelet at top of long flight of steps)

Best Beaches

Archirondel – top of beach stony
Beauport – (but steep path)
Bonne Nuit – actually a fishing harbour, picturesque
Grève de Lecq – best on north coast
Plémont – sandy cove, rock pools for young children
Portelet – lots of steps but worth it
Royal Bay of Grouville – miles of sand

Swimming around Jersey

Sea bathing in Jersey is a great attraction, and it is the most varied in the British Isles. However, moderate swimmers and more especially non-swimmers should exercise reasonable care so as to ensure complete safety when bathing. The following bays are suggested:

Non-Swimmers
Grève d'Azette, St Catherine, St Clement, St Aubin, Grouville, St Brelade and Anne Port.

Moderate Swimmers
The bays mentioned plus Fliquet, Bonne Nuit, Rozel, Grève de Lecq, Bouley, Plémont, Giffard and Portelet.

Strong Swimmers
All the bays previously mentioned, plus St Ouen. The last mentioned is unequalled for its surf bathing but, owing to the undercurrent, *experienced swimmers only* should engage in this sport.

Bathing is dangerous when the red cone is flying; safe bathing area is between red and yellow flags.

The coastline of Jersey experiences one of the largest movements of tide recorded in the world. The vertical rise of tide between low water mark and high water mark during periods of spring tides can be as much as 40ft (12m). During the third and fourth hours of a rising spring tide, the rate of rise can be as much as 2in (5cm) per minute. These large tides cause strong tidal currents around the coastline and adjacent waters and care must be exercised by visitors when swimming or exploring the rocky foreshore, although of course, the bays indicated are quite safe for the type of swimming mentioned.

The Tourism Committee employs a fully professional team of Beach Guards who man the modern lifesaving centre at St Ouen's Bay, and also keep watch at St Brelade's Bay, Plémont and West Park, maintaining constant communication with HQ by means of radio telephone. Beach Guard Service, end of May to 1 October from 10am–6pm every day, ☎ St Ouen's Bay 482032, Plémont Bay 481636.

Jersey Produce

Tucked away in the north-west of the island in St Mary is La Mare Vineyard. Working with 21 acres of vines, excellent wines are being produced here together with apple brandy, distilled on site, and cider. With the growing demand for speciality preserves, mustards and chutney, a wide variety of these in matching jars are also now being produced.

Each year, between 30,000–40,000 bottles of wine rattle along the production line with over 100 tons of apples being picked for bottle conditioned vintage cider and Jersey apple bandy. The latter is aged in oak casks to create the soft and mellow tasting spirit. It is one of the very few places in Britain with a licence to distil apple brandy.

Apple crushing for Cider production.

The wines include award-winning sparkling wines, dry and medium-dry whites and 'Bailiwick' red wine.

Additionally, La Mare produce excellent marmalades, jams, jellies and mustards along with Jersey fudge and speciality chocolates. Another speciality well worth trying is Jersey black butter. It is nothing like traditional butter, however. It is made from cider, spices and treacle rendered down to a thick and delicious-tasting spread.

The company has a shop in King Street, St Helier where they also sell other Jersey products including Jersey pottery, candles, soap and cream liqueur.

South of St Mary parish is St Peter and close to the centre of the village is Classic Herd Ltd. Here Jersey cheeses are being made. The farm shop is now selling Camembert and Brie cheeses, with home-produced meats too. Look out for the Jersey cow on the label!

Look out too for locally caught fish, delicious oysters harvested chiefly for the French market and, more unusually, ormers. Half a dozen oysters and

a pint of beer make a good combination. The Tipsy Toad Brewery, set up in the 1990s, has more recently amalgamated with the existing Jersey Brewery. Their range of beers are available on draught all around the island and are well worth looking out for. Flying Flowers and Sunset Flowers both export flowers but also sell them locally and by mail order.

Beauport Bay.

Islands – after Churchill decided they could not be defended and declared them demilitarised. The bunkers and the gun emplacements were constructed on Hitler's orders to make Jersey part of an impregnable fortress against the enemy – the British. Some of them, together with the German Underground Hospital, are open to the public who want to know more about the almost 5 years of German occupation, when the islanders suffered such great deprivation, and came near to starvation before the long-awaited Liberation Day, 9 May 1945.

The Government of Jersey

A fact of which all islanders are justifiably proud is that Jersey's internal affairs have never been administered by Parliament in Westminster. Jersey has, since the time of King John, always had independent home rule, while larger issues, such as the ratification of laws and foreign policy, are dealt with by the Queen and her Privy Council. The important link between the island and the United Kingdom is through the Crown. Its two representatives in Jersey are the Bailiff – a Jerseyman who usually comes to the office through the island's legal system – and the Lieutenant-Governor, a member of the British Armed Forces, whose term of appointment is five years. The Bailiff takes precedence in the States Assembly, the island's government, and the Royal Court, the island's supreme court, while the Lieutenant-Governor, who is the island's commander-in-chief, takes precedence elsewhere.

The States, when in session, normally sit in their chamber in the Royal Square every alternate Tuesday and their debates can be heard from the public gallery. The fifty-three honorary members, under the presidency of the Bailiff, comprise twelve Senators, the twelve parish Constables and twenty-nine Deputies – all elected on non-party political platforms to serve terms of office from three to six years. From their number committees are drawn up to put forward policies on such aspects of island life as education, finance, social security and tourism. Once approved by the States, their directives are carried out by a staff of civil servants.

The Royal Court, the island's court of justice, is made up of the Bailiff and twelve honorary, elected judges, known as Jurats. They hear the civil and criminal cases brought before them, which are of too serious a nature to be dealt with by the magistrate's court, in the Royal Court Chamber in the Royal Square. The Royal Court is also the island's court of appeal. Anyone wishing to take his case further has then to ask leave to appeal to the judicial committee of the Privy Council. Stipendiary magistrates, members of the legal profession, preside over the magistrates and petty debts courts. Visitors may attend the sittings of the Royal Court but it is not generally open to visitors.

Local as opposed to central government in Jersey is administered through the Parish Assembly in each of the twelve parishes. It is presided over by the Connétable, or Constable, the most important man in the parish, whose honorary elected position dates back at least to the fifteenth-century. Its members include Centeniers, Vingteniers, the Constable's Officers, and the Procureurs du Bien Public, who decide such matters within the parish boundaries as finance, rates, parking and the social welfare of their parishioners.

The Constable also heads the non-uniformed honorary police force in his parish – the Centeniers, Vingteniers and Constable's Officers – but is in no way the equivalent of an English constable. The Centeniers carry a warrant and have the power to order an enquiry into traffic accidents and institute criminal proceedings. So, for example, should a visitor be involved in an infringement of the traffic regulations outside St Helier, the incident could be dealt with on the spot by the honorary police of the parish where it took place, or at a subsequent parish hall enquiry.

Centeniers are helped in their duties by the Vingteniers and Constable's Officers and work in close conjunction with the island's uniformed police force who have their headquarters in Rouge Bouillon, St Helier.

Facilities for the Holidaymaker

Jersey is not just an island for basking on the beach in the sun, attractive and varied as its beaches are, for there are so many other activities on offer for the holidaymaker to enjoy.

Indoors

Art exhibitions are held in galleries throughout the island and, in the summer, even in the Royal Square itself. Plays and concerts – from classical to pop – are held in the large Gloucester Hall in Fort Regent, the Opera House which dates back to 1900, or the Benjamin Meaker Theatre in the Arts Centre.

Cineworld, the island's ten-screen cinema, often features top pre-release films at the same time as West End openings, with tickets at a fraction of London prices. Many restaurants and pubs have live entertainment, so there are plenty of opportunities to enjoy an evening watching a cabaret turn, joining in a sing-along, taking part in a talent contest or listening to country and western, rock, pop or folk music. There are also venues for nightclubs and ballroom dancing. Licensing hours are at the discretion of the proprietor.

For book lovers, the two libraries, one in St Helier, the other in St Brelade, will lend books to visitors on payment of a returnable deposit, or in exchange for their usual library card. Both libraries have a children's section.

Out of Doors

To begin with, there are all the water sports from sailing to scuba diving, with windsurfing and surfing two of the most popular. Fishing can be carried on the whole year with, for example, pollock to be caught when sea temperatures are at their lowest in January, February and March, ling prolific in high summer and large size mackerel among many other fish to be caught in the last three months of the year. For freshwater fishermen there are opportunities for both fly and coarse fishing.

Land sports include golf, tennis, climbing, horse riding and walking. The island has six golf courses including three 18-hole course for visitors who are members of a recognised golf club, two public golf courses, and three venues where mini-golf can be enjoyed. There are sixteen public hard tennis courts, three bowling clubs, a croquet club, a newly formed climbing association, plus at least four riding stables which welcome visitors. Cliff paths for the keen walker stretch from Grosnez Castle in the north-west to Rozel in the north-east – a stretch of more than 20 miles (32.25km).

For those interested in history there are several museums, two castles, a couple of manor houses and German Occupation relics to be visited, as well as guided tours to be joined.

For the nature lover there is the natural flora and fauna of the island to enjoy, from the yellow lent lilies (*Narcissus pseudonarcissus*) in the spring to the pink Jersey lily (*Amaryllis belladonna*) in the autumn, while the cliff tops are covered in yellow gorse for most of the year. To the west of the island there is The Frances Le Sueur Centre, near Kempt Tower with all the information about the island's only designated conservation area, Les Mielles, a sand dune landscape of

Jersey has an extensive cycle network.

ecological importance; to the north-east there are the exotic, richly perfumed orchid blooms of the Eric Young Foundation Centre. In the spring, birdwatchers can see brent geese feeding at the water's edge and in the woods hear or catch sight of a blackcap or great spotted woodpecker. Puffins, shags and fulmars can be spotted on inaccessible cliff ledges along the north coast. For visitors who just prefer sitting, there are several public parks, including Howard Davis Park in St Saviour, where visiting bands play during the summer months.

Floral floats parade, Battle of the Flowers

Family Attractions & Entertainment

Battle of Flowers Museum

Le Mont des Corvées, St Ouen

☎ 01534 730178

www.battleofflowers.com

The museum houses the exclusive collection of floats designed and made by Florence Bechelet. They have all competed in the annual Battle of the Flowers, a highlight in Jersey's calendar. This important tradition takes place in early August. The floats are mainly made using the dried heads of mare's tail grasses. These are dyed and glued onto a frame. They are amazing creations and do have to be seen to be appreciated. So many mare's tails are used that they are grown specially near to the museum.

Open: 10am–5pm; Apr to Oct

Discovery Pier

Gorey Pier, St Martin

☎ 01534 617704

www.durrell.org

This attraction brings together on shore Jersey's rich marine ecology for visitors to experience.

The wildlife of wrecks is shown on DVD; interactive fun for youngsters, including a working rock pool; record breaking fish; how the tides work and two full size bottle-nosed dolphins are just an example of things to entertain.

Open: 11am – 3pm, May to Sept.

Durrell Wildlife

Les Augrès Manor, Trinity

☎ 01534 860000

Jersey's famed animal sanctuary. Dozens of species from across the world in settings close to their natural habitat.

Open: 9.30am–5pm, daily (until 6pm in summer).

Elizabeth Castle

St Aubin's Bay, St Helier

☎ 01534 633376

A trip to Elizabeth Castle is made more exciting by arriving by ferry. Arrive by midday to view and hear the 'Call to Arms' by the duty gunner. The signal gun is fired daily at the end of the interactive presentation. (approx. 12.45pm).

Open: Apr to mid-Oct

Hamptonne Country Life Museum

La Rue de la Patente, St Lawrence

☎ 01534 633300

Visitors to Hamptonne are informed about farm life in the 16th century. Chickens and geese roam freely at this restored farm complex. There is plenty of space for children to wander and explore. They will be able to stroke friendly horses and calves, see cows in the meadow and pigs in the sty. There is also a children's play area and a number of outdoor games. There are also exhibitions: one tells the story of the filming of 'Under the Greenwood Tree' that was filmed at Hamptonne and another tells the story of the Jersey cow.

Open: daily; Apr to Nov

Jersey Pottery

Gorey village, Grouville

☎ 01534 850850

www.jerseypottery.com

Jersey Pottery is a commercial pottery where you can see all stages of production.

Children and adults can personalise their own pottery.

Open: 9am – 5.30pm, Mon to Sat, 10am – 5.30pm Sun

Jersey War Tunnels

Les Charrieres, Malory, St Lawrence

☎ 01534 860808

www.jerseywartunnels.com

The German occupation of Jersey is told in a unique way. It aims to place the visitor in the shoes of those who experienced this period, making the visit more interesting, especially for children.

It is based in tunnels and takes you from captivity and siege through to liberation.

Open: 10am–6pm daily

Feb to Nov

La Hougue Bie

Grouville

☎ 01534 633373

Older than the pyramids of Egypt, this 13m high mound is topped by a medieval chapel. Deep inside the 6,000-year-old mound lies one of Europe's finest Neolithic dolmens.

Younger visitors enjoy the activities within a reconstructed Neolithic house that brings the Stone Age alive.

Open: Apr to early Nov

Living Legend

La Rue du Petit Aleval, St Peter

☎ 01534 485496

www.jerseylivinglegend.co.je

This is a village attraction offering fantastic fun for all the family. It includes a dynamic multimedia presentation and exhibition of Jersey's history. Explore myths and legends in the dungeons or travel undersea on a voyage of discovery, described as magical and unforgettable.

Outside there are numerous activities for the children, including go-karting, golf, adventure playground, indoor crèche.

The adventure golf course covers 3 acres and is surrounded by beautiful gardens.

A choice of eating establishments make it possible to stay for the day. There is also an ice cream parlour and fudge kitchen.

Maritime Museum & Occupation Tapestry Gallery

New North Quay, St Helier

☎ 01534 633372

Exciting, fun and interactive. Create your own waves, watch craftsmen work on classic boats, design your own ship and experience the life of a sailor. Described as brilliant and entertaining for the whole family.

The Occupation Tapestry Gallery tells the story of life in Jersey during World War II. It is a community work and captures islanders' personal memories.

Open: 10am – 4pm daily

aMaizin Maze

La Grande Route de St Pierre, St Peter

☎ 01534 482116

www.jerseymaze.com

This is an award-winning family attraction. Children love the freedom of the adventure park, amaizin barnyard, toboggan run, 9-hole crazy golf course, giant sand pit, daily parrot show, tractor rides and much more.

Open: end Apr to mid-Sept

Mont Orgueil

☎ 01534 633375

Gorey, St Martin

One of the best-preserved castles in Britain. An understanding of its history is made interesting by the fascinating exhibition that is portrayed throughout the site.

Giant sculptures include a 'wound man', a figure from a medieval surgeon's almanac demonstrating various types of battle wounds; most gruesome and therefore captivating to younger audiences! Equally morbid is a tree of life festooned with dozens of staring heads.

Cylindrical World War II observation towers can be seen on the roof of the castle and of course the splendid view of the bay and the

French coast.

Open: 10am–6pm, daily, Apr to Nov.

Nov to Dec 10am–dusk, Fri, Sat, Sun, Mon

**Pallot Steam, Motor
& General Museum**

La Rue de Bechet, Trinity

☎ 01534 865307

www.pallotmuseum.co.uk

This fascinating private collection of steam engines, cars and a variety of other machinery will interest and occupy adults and children too. Lots to see. There are also steam and diesel train rides.

Open: 10am–5pm (not Sundays)

April to end Oct

Samarès Manor also **Jersey Rural
Life & Carriage Museum**

St Clement

☎ 01534 870551

This fine example of a manor house is open to the public. A fascinating story is told of its history to the present day.

There are gardens to enjoy and guided tours. Samarès Manor is home to Jersey's Rural Life & Carriage Museum. The visitor can view a wide range of agricultural equipment, carts and carriages, learning of a time when farming was a craft. The exhibits ensure that Jersey's agricultural heritage is not forgotten.

Open: 9.30am – 5pm daily, April to mid-Oct

Parks with Play Areas

Les Jardin de la Mer

Waterfront, St Helier

These are maritime gardens with an illuminated water maize at night. An activity centre is nearby with trampolines and skatepark.

Coronation Park

Millbrook, St Lawrence

Beautiful gardens, children's play area and paddling pool. There is easy access to the beach and promenade of St Aubins Bay.

Howard Davis Park

St Saviour

Lovely gardens, large park and playground.

People's Park

Westmount, St Helier

Outskirts of town with small playground.

Parade Gardens

The Parade, St Helier

Within walking distance of town centre. Safe enclosed playground.

Baby changing facilities

St Helier

A de Gruchy

King Street. Nursery Dept

Mothercare

Charing Cross. Parents room available

BHS

King Street, 1st Floor. Provision for nursing, café available

Boots

Queen Street. Lower sales floor

M & S

King Street. First floor, near Customer Services

Pushchair hire

Zebra Cycle Hire

☎ 01534 736556

The Hire Shop

☎ 01534 873699

1. St Helier

Around St Helier

Despite its present size and importance as the capital of Jersey, St Helier was not always the centre of island affairs as it is today. For one thing, the island's only castle in medieval times was Gorey Castle, in the parish of St Martin, and from it the island was governed for several centuries; for another, the most sheltered and easily accessible port was at St Aubin, in the parish of St Brelade, while St Helier harbour was not completed as a commercial port until well into the nineteenth-century.

The earliest settlement in the eastern corner of St Aubin's Bay, probably in the sixth-century, was on a marshy plain between Mont Millais in the east, Westmount in the west and Mont au Prêtre in the north.

The settlement also included the rocky outcrop jutting out into the sea towards the south-east, where Fort Regent now stands.

The whole area was named after the saint who for 15 years lived the life of a hermit on the small islet just south of this marshy coast, whose martyrdom has given the present town its emblem of two axes.

Many legends have been told about St Helier himself, but it is known that he was born in Tongres in Belgium and that he came to Jersey in about AD540. It is said that his pagan parents had named him Helibert, but that after he had been cured of paralysis at the age of 7 by the Christian missionary Cunibert, he was called Helier, which means pity, because God had obviously taken pity on him.

When Helier grew up, he served as a missionary under St Marculf, who had a Christian centre at Nanteuil, and it was St Marculf who suggested that Helier came to live and preach in Jersey. When Helier arrived, the settlement on the marsh numbered only about thirty people.

They were probably mostly fishermen, and he decided to minister to their spiritual needs from a small cell he built on a high rock about 1.5miles (2.4km) from the coast, quite surrounded by the sea at high tide and reached at low tide by a natural causeway.

The site of the cell, and the oratory afterwards built on L'Islet, is known today as the **Hermitage Rock**.

Tradition has it that from that natural vantage point of his hermit's cell, St Helier was able for 15 years, with God's help, to keep marauding Norman raiders from attacking and stealing from his small flock.

At last, however, the legend tells of how in that fifteenth year some of the Norman raiders, despite being blown out to sea by an offshore wind through the prayers of Helier, did manage to land. When they saw Helier praying alone on the seashore they swung their axes against him and cut off his head.

In Helier's memory, St Marculf founded a monastery on the islet where he had lived for the 15 years of his ministry – where Elizabeth Castle now stands. Today, in memory of St Helier, a pilgrimage – led by the dean and clergy of Jersey and the Constable of St Helier - is made on the Sunday nearest to 16 July, tide permitting, to the Hermitage Rock and any visitor is welcome to join in.

The history of L'Islet 400 years after St Helier's death is a chequered one, because in another Norman raid in the tenth-century the monastery of St Helier founded by St Marculf was sacked and destroyed.

It remained in ruins until a wealthy man in Normandy, in whose dukedom Jersey then was, decided in about 1125 to build an abbey in its place. Fifty years or so later the abbey was demoted to become a priory but still had to pay revenues to Normandy.

A priory it remained until Henry V of England (for by this time Jersey owed allegiance to the English Crown) confiscated all property belonging to priories held by foreigners. Without its wealth, which had been considerable, the priory could not carry on and soon fell into disrepair.

When Queen Elizabeth I's military engineer, Paul Ivy, came to Jersey in 1594 to update the island's defences, he immediately saw L'Islet with its ruined priory as the obvious site for a new castle. When it was completed in about 1600, official documents named it the New Castle; local inhabitants called it Le Château de L'Islet; today it is known simply as **Elizabeth Castle**. So any of the thousands of holidaymakers who visit it every year are not only looking over a sixteenth-century castle but are also walking over the site – in the great courtyard of the castle – of a Christian centre which remained an important force for the religious instruction and secular organisation of islanders for over 400 years.

There are two ways to get to Elizabeth Castle, both starting from the slipway at West Park. One is to walk a mile (1.6km) along the causeway from the slipway, which is dry enough to use for about 5 hours between high tides; the second is to use the regular ferry service. Visitors who want to walk back to the mainland are informed by staff half an hour before the causeway is due to be covered, which can be by as much as 15ft (4.5m) of water on a high spring tide.

The first gate of Elizabeth Castle the visitor passes through is guarded on the west side by Fort Charles and on the east by the north-east bastion.

The bell in the belfry above the gate is the one which gives half an hour's warning of the incoming tide. Admission to the castle is by the main gate and is in the old port guard house.

The second gate leads to the first of the three sections into which the castle is divided – the outer ward. This owes much of its strength to the fact that the castle's original builders made good use of the rocks that projected naturally round the edge of the narrow islet, thereby also giving the sentries guarding the landward side of the castle an uninterrupted view of its walls right round to the central lower ward. Within the outer ward, around the green, were erected, in the 1700s, such necessary buildings to a garrison force as a lime-kiln, stables, workshops, general store and even a hospital.

The castle's third gate leads from the outer ward to the more important lower ward. Here are the barracks, the officers' quarters, the canteen and cook houses, the early eighteenth-century gymnasium, now a militia museum, storerooms and the seventeenth-century magazine, in the south-west corner of the ward. Visitors will also notice the huge iron water storage tanks which were the only way to ensure a fresh supply of water for the garrison before 1874, when a mains water pipe from the town was finally laid.

The iron gate, with its typical Jersey granite arch, the fourth gate through which the visitor passes, leads to the oldest part of the castle, the upper ward, the only part of the rock fortified by Ivy, Queen Elizabeth's chief engineer. This was originally guarded in Elizabethan times by fifteen cannon. The fifth and final gate, named after the Queen, is arguably the most architecturally perfect of them all. Visitors can see not just the coat of arms of the English Queen on the gate but also, to the left, the arms of Jersey's Governor from 1590 to1600, Sir Anthony Poulet. For in the upper ward or keep was built the Governor's house, first lived in by Sir Walter Raleigh, when he was the island's Governor from 1600 until 1603, after which he was deprived of his governorship by James II and imprisoned in the Tower of London. Now this typically seventeenth-century Jersey granite house is where visitors can see an Exhibition Gallery depicting some of the famous events which took place in the castle during the several centuries of its development.

There was the siege of the newly-enlarged castle during the English Civil War when, in 1645, the Parliamentary Lieutenant-Governor Major Lydcott unsuccessfully besieged the Royalist Sir Philippe de Carteret. Three years later, the fleeing Prince of Wales, later to become Charles II, took refuge in the castle from his father's enemies for 10 weeks. He returned to Jersey as the newly proclaimed king in 1649, staying 20 weeks. After the restoration of the monarchy, Charles gave land in America to Sir George Carteret as an expression of his regard for his loyalty to him and his father. This land was named New Jersey.

Whilst Charles was in the castle, eleven people suffering from the skin complaint scrofula went for a healing session in the old abbey church where it was said that just a touch from King Charles and the words 'May God heal thee' cured them of their disease immediately.

Then for the 9 years between 1651 and 1660, Royalist sympathisers had to lie low in Jersey, for the island Governors who lived in Elizabeth Castle during that time were all Cromwell's men. The castle's next excitement was over a hundred years later, when the French adventurer, de Rullecourt, invaded Jersey in 1781. As he rode out with his forces from St Helier and along the causeway to demand the surrender of the castle, the only reply he got was cannon fire, one ball amputating the leg of one of his officers. So de Rullecourt wisely decided to retire. With the victory of Major Peirson later in the day, no further action from the castle was needed.

The breakwater which joins the upper ward to the Hermitage Rock and St Helier's Oratory was a nineteenth century attempt to give the town of St Helier a proper harbour. The arm which juts out nearly 700yd (640m) further into the sea was designed to meet a similar arm from La Collette. But as this was smashed by south-westerly gales 3 years running, the whole idea of the new harbour was eventually abandoned.

When the Germans occupied Jersey, in 1940–5, Elizabeth Castle had its final reconstruction as a fortress. Visitors will notice in the outer ward the concrete base in the centre of Fort Charles' tower where a gun was positioned, and the underground shelter near the hospital; in the lower ward, the machine gun and floodlight post on the green bastion, together with the one gun casemate, for which part of the eighteenth-century canteen was demolished. In the upper ward no one can fail to notice the

Elizabeth Castle, firing the midday gun and the parade ground.

concrete fire-control tower which is so ill-matched with the seventeenth-century keep, the original of the castle which Sir Walter Raleigh proudly named 'Fort Isabella Bellissima', the 'castle of Elizabeth the most beautiful'.

Such have been the efforts in recent years to restore this historic monument set so magnificently in St Aubin's Bay that in 1987 Elizabeth Castle was awarded a Civic Trust commendation. So holidaymakers will find a visit not only enjoyable but informative as well. There is, for example, an exhibition called 'Granite and Gunpowder'. In the Barracks opposite are tableaux tracing the whole 400-year-long history of armaments and fortifications used to defend the island. Visitors should be ready, by the way, if in the vicinity of the castle at noon or shortly after to put their hands over their ears – for that is when one of the guns at the castle is fired in

a daily salute!

Because of the number of stone steps within the castle precincts, it is unfortunately limited for visitors with impaired mobility.

On the opposite side of the harbour from the castle the view is dominated by the rocky ridge that cuts through the middle of St Helier, now surmounted by a spaceage dome but originally the site of another piece of Jersey's military heritage.

This large fort, took eight years to build, just a year before Napoleon's defeat at Waterloo. It was named after the Prince Regent, later to become George IV and is still known today, though in quite a different context, as **Fort Regent**. Visitors to it will see how skilfully its builders have used the rock of Le Mont de la Ville to make the fortress impregnable and what a vantage point there is to be had from any of its ramparts. It did not, however, serve the defence purpose for which it was originally built – despite its having the most up-to-date design in fortifications at the time of its building and being continuously garrisoned by units of the British Army until 1927 – until 120 years after its completion. This was when the Germans used Fort Regent as an ordnance depot and sited anti-aircraft guns on its summit to be fired against British and Allied aircraft.

The British government sold Fort Regent back to the States of Jersey in 1958 – for just £3,220 more than they had bought it from St Helier in 1804. Then came the problem of what to do with a Napoleonic fortress which had outlived its usefulness. Nine years later, in 1967, it was decided – after much heated debate – to convert Fort Regent into a leisure centre providing amenities for both residents and tourists. So now,

in the unique setting of a nineteenth-century fortification, with panoramic views over the sea and the town, there is a leisure complex that includes everything from concerts and conferences to swimming and sports, making the Fort the premier Leisure Centre in Jersey.

Access to Fort Regent is either by the stone steps in Pier Road for the energetic, or there are lifts and escalators in the adjacent multi-storey car park. In the Fort there is a diverse range of leisure facilities and attractions for all ages. Children will love the indoor and outdoor adventure playgrounds, both with sections for the under fives. For the sports enthusiast there is the chance to try something new or to have a game of an old favourite: the range indoors includes bowls, table tennis, snooker, badminton and squash – and there are changing and shower facilities. Those who have come

Elizabeth Castle, with some of its cannon.

to Jersey to get or keep fit will want to find their way to the weight training and fitness rooms in Jersey's largest Health and Fitness Centre, 'Jungle Gym' and crèche for younger children.

The 2,000-seater auditorium of the Gloucester Hall is the venue for some fifteen concerts and shows a year, covering pop, classical and comedy. Three or four exhibitions are staged here, such as the craft fair in September.

As the Gloucester Hall also makes a perfect conference hall – every year Jersey hosts at least one or two conferences of over 1,000 delegates and several smaller ones – just opposite is the Don Theatre Conference Suite, with a 150-seater audio-visual theatre, plus a room suitable for receptions and another for board meetings.

In between the Piazza and the Gloucester Hall there is the Queen's Hall which has been built over the former parade ground. This huge area of 16,000sq ft1,500m²) below the dome of the roof provides a wide range of sports and other leisure activities. The Queen's Hall also gives a permanent home to the Compton cinema organ which used to be in the now demolished Forum Cinema. To complete the attractions of Queen's Hall, a balcony goes right round it at rampart level with space for exhibitions, lounges and viewing areas. There is also a rose garden for a relaxing stroll, or a picnic with a panoramic view over the ramparts.

There are bars serving pub meals, snack bars and a restaurant, all within the complex.

The Town of St Helier

Between the time of St Helier in the sixth-century and General Don in the nineteenth, the development of the town was a surprisingly slow one. Until the Middle Ages there was still only a small community of fishermen living near the shore, with two small chapels for worship: the earliest, La Chapelle de la Madelaine, just north-west of where the present parish church is now, and La Chapelle de Notre Dame des Pas on the eastern slope of Le Mont de la Ville, near the sea end of Green Street. The town's turning point only came when the monks of the abbey on L'Islet obtained a royal licence to hold a market in St Helier, where the Royal Square is now.

Then, where the farmers congregated every market day, usually a Saturday, first taverns and then shops were built for their convenience. Later still, the growing St Helier was found to be more central than Gorey for the hearing of court cases, so a primitive Royal Court was built next to the marketplace. However, there were, in the fourteenth-century, still fewer people living in St Helier than in the country parishes of St Saviour, Grouville, St Martin, Trinity or even St Ouen. In 1593 there were still only 300 households in the town.

Until as late as the eighteenth-century the extent of St Helier from east to west was marked by its pumps: La Pompe de Bas at Charing Cross and La Pompe du Haut at Snow Hill. To the south of these two landmarks was La Muraille de la Ville, the town wall, built in a vain endeavour to stop sand from the dunes to the south getting into the streets and shops of the town. Behind La Rue du Milieu, now Queen Street, and La Rue de Derrière, now King Street, were only gardens and fields.

An extremely narrow strip of a town and, apparently, none too clean: Sir Walter Raleigh, from his experience of being the island's Governor for 3 years, spoke of St Helier as a 'mean and dirty place'. Eighty years later a special official was appointed to keep the town clean, but still complaints were made about the filthy state of the streets – in which much more than litter was deposited – and about pigs running loose round the Market Place and through the nearby cemetery. The present-day Church Street was called La Rue Trousse Cotillon (Tuck Up Your Petticoat Street) because to go along its dirty length ladies had to tuck up their skirts!

In 1685, when the revocation of the Edict of Nantes meant the persecution of Huguenots in France once more, many fled to French-speaking Jersey and no doubt accounted in some measure for the increase in the population of St Helier to 5–6,000. Another influx of French refugees, this time political, came with the French Revolution, so that by 1800 the population of the town was about 8,000.

Most of the fine, large buildings of the present town, therefore, were not put up and the harbour not built until the nineteenth-century. In fact, the accessibility and size of St Helier's harbour had a great deal to do with the growth of the town. Only in 1700 was the first small harbour built, known as La Folie and hence the name of the pub (closed in 2004, but due for redevelopment) that

overlooked it; the extensions to it, of the New North Quay and South Pier, came over a hundred years later in 1813. But even these were unable to cope with the great number of Jersey ships involved at this time in the Newfoundland fishing trade, so the States decided to treble the harbour's size. One of the first people to step ashore on the new south pier in 1846 was the young Queen Victoria, and it was named Victoria Pier. Her husband's name of Albert was given to the second, north pier, completed in 1853.

Despite these enlargements of the harbour, the central problem of the town's port still remained – at low tide it had not sufficient water for ships to enter! In fact, when the royal couple landed, Prince Albert asked, 'Why do you Jerseymen always build your harbours on dry land?'

In the 1990s there were further extensions to the harbour to accommodate today's larger container ships and car ferries.

The Marina

Built for smaller craft is the **St Helier Marina**. Conveniently placed in the Upper Harbour, opposite the harbour office, this Marina is, literally, only a few minutes from the town centre.

Opened in 1981, this Marina provides permanent berths for about 180 local craft, leaving 200 berths for visitors. Approaches to St Helier are described in detail in the following Admiralty Charts: 3655, 1137 and 3278; and visiting craft should keep a listening watch on Channel 14 VHF, *not* Channel M, when approaching. You will find that all your needs are met within the Marina complex. Fresh water is laid on to all pontoons and, providing that there is a suitable point, electric power can be supplied. An amenity block on the New North Quay houses toilets, showers, laundry and telephones. The Marina shop, with a full range of provisions, is open all year.

During July and August the demand for berths can exceed supply, so it is wise before crossing the sea to Jersey to check by telephone or radio to make sure that a berth is available. Advance bookings cannot be made. Once here, visiting yachtsmen will receive a warm welcome at either St Helier Yacht Club, on the South Pier, or the Royal Channel Islands Yacht Club, at the Bulwarks, St Aubin.

The Elizabeth Marina has 564 berths. Long-stay visitors who are staying in the marina for one month or more will be directed to this marina, while short-stay visitors will continue to be moored in the town Marina.

For those without boats of their own, there are several possibilities. At the kiosk at the north end of the Albert Pier bookings are taken for *Southern Bay Rose*. She has a lounge bar, sun and shelter decks and starts to cruise along Jersey's picturesque southern coast at 11am and at 2pm daily (11am only, Mon, Wed and Fri in July and August).

Shopping In St Helier

Many visitors comment on the town's fresh, clean appearance and they crowd its streets looking for items that are both different from back home and, because VAT does not apply in Jersey, often at least 17½ per cent cheaper.

St Helier is made even more attractive by the numerous first-class restaurants, inexpensive cafés and snack bars – often with tables outside – and public houses. Bands sometimes march through the streets of the town, and colourful street entertainers often perform in the town's pedestrianised precincts.

Most of St Helier's shops are in the pedestrian precinct of Queen Street and King Street, which runs east from Snow Hill and westwards towards Charing Cross. The chief shopping streets coming into the precinct from the north, are – starting at Snow Hill – Bath Street, Halkett Place and New Street. To the south of the precinct are the Royal Square and the States Offices, Conway Street and Broad Street, where there is the General Post Office. There is plenty to delight the visitor, though, who wanders away from the pedestrian precinct and main shopping area to explore the many little byways that go to make up St Helier.

The best bargains to be found in St Helier are perfume, cosmetics, jewellery, cigarettes and tobacco, alcohol, electrical goods, cameras, watches, sports equipment, china and glass – all because they are VAT-free and almost duty-free as well. So the visitors should not be surprised at the number of shops they see specialising solely in cosmetics, toiletries and perfume – all at less than the UK price. Even more noticeable are the number of shops selling watches and jewellery, again at competitive prices, which fall even lower during the winter, for off-season visitors to take advantage of. Not only is there new as well as antique jewellery on offer in St Helier, but there is at least one jeweller in town who will

Elizabeth Marina and Fort Regent.

make items to suit the customer's own individual requirements.

When it comes to buying clothes, not only will holidaymakers find the shops they are used to in their own High Street on the mainland, but also individual and specialist boutiques for every member of the family. There are plenty of places selling fashionable smart and leisure clothing. There are also two first-rate department stores situated in the pedestrian precinct. Many of the shops in St Helier have been run by Jersey families for several decades, all of them offering friendly service, as well as the best of local, English and Continental goods.

When it comes to hunting for souvenirs or presents, the most popular are those with a local flavour. So look out for silver spoons which bear the parish crest, copper milk cans and churns, miniature reminders of how milk used to be collected on Jersey farms, sets of local coins and stamps. Also available are items made by local artists and craftsmen, such as paintings, pottery, wooden artefacts and the warm oiled-wool sweater, the genuine Jersey.

Waterfront.

Leisure Activities

St Helier Waterfront is Jersey's newest leisure development and incorporates a ten-screen multiplex cinema, water park, fitness centre, bar, nightclub and restaurants set within a modern architectural and landscaped environment.

Football fans will enjoy watching the island's principal matches up at Springfield but the event which commands the largest crowds there is the Muratti, a competition between Jersey, Guernsey and Alderney. When the final is held in Jersey, it takes place in early May. The

Springfield Stadium was specially built in time for the 1997 Island Games, which were hosted by Jersey.

Dining out is a must, as there is so much to tempt both the gourmet and the family who want a cheap meal. Diners will find restaurants specialising in French, Italian, Portuguese, Greek, Chinese, Indian and even Malayan dishes. There are those, too, which offer more traditional English fare, but a feature of most eating places is their use of fresh local produce, such as Jersey Royal potatoes, cauliflower and tomatoes and, in particular, locally caught seafood. Many visitors comment with amazement that their excellent meal has cost them only about half of what a similar meal in the UK would have done.

Live shows can be enjoyed at either the Opera House or the Arts Centre throughout the year, either put on by local artistes or professional UK performers. These range from concerts and cabarets to full length plays. There are also plenty of other musical events throughout the year, from amateur recitals to festivals.

Those who enjoy nightlife will find traditional pubs and trendy new bars in St Helier as well as several night-clubs including the Liquid Nightclub, which plays chart and dance, R and B and Funky House in the lounge bar, open 10pm–late.

Details of where to eat and what to do in St Helier on any night of your holiday can be found in the leisure pages of the *Jersey Evening Post*, which is on sale from mid-afternoon, giving plenty of time to make a choice.

Throughout the year various festivals take place in St Helier, some of them transforming the streets of the town, such as the Good Food Festival, which takes place at the end of May.

Other nationalities also have their own festivals, such as the Irish, Scottish and Portuguese Festivals.

In July and August, flowers are the theme in St Helier. In July is Floral Island Week, during which shops, banks, hotels and private houses and flats in town compete against one another in a floral competition, beautifying St Helier in the process. Then, of course, at the beginning of August is Jersey's Battle of Flowers. The floral floats parade up and down Victoria Avenue, delighting the crowds that line both sides. Even taxis and coaches are decorated on the Thursday of the Battle of Flowers!

At the end of the year comes the town's final transformation – at Christmas. A huge tree is placed in the Royal Square, together with a nativity tableau, and the lights and decorations strung across the streets and the precinct make a veritable fairyland of St Helier after dark. Carols are sung in the Royal Square, the market and the pedestrian precinct to complete the yuletide scene.

Tours of St Helier

For those interested in historic places and buildings in St Helier, here are four short tours of the town, each one starting from a different car park, beginning with Green Street in the east and finishing with Patriotic Street in the west. Bus users who come to St Helier's terminus (also site of the Tourist Information Centre) can join or walk to the start of any tour from there. In general terms, as has been seen, most of the old buildings in St Helier date only from the nineteenth-century, but even where modern shop fronts line the streets a glance above could reveal interesting architecture from another age, often with a distinct French influence. Visitors might also find the tours more useful if they read them first in their hotel or guest house before starting out.

A number of professional tour guides, who have won their coveted 'Blue Badge' awards, run special tours through the streets of the town. For details about time and availability ☎ 01534 500700

1 Green Street north To La Colomberie Or south To Havre Des Pas

Turning north and then east from the car park just beyond where Green Street makes the fork with Grenville Street, is **Green Street cemetery**. Not only is this a peaceful place to sit, but it also has a memorial at its southern end to the only St Helier official to be killed in the course of doing his duty. The 25ft (7.6m)-high granite monument was erected by the citizens of St Helier to the memory of Centenier George Le Cronier.

With the Constable's Officer, he had gone on 28 February 1846 to arrest a couple in Patriotic Street for keeping a house of ill repute. When the two men arrived at the house, only the wife was at home but, as the Centenier was about to arrest her, she suddenly took up a carving knife and thrust it into Le Cronier's stomach. The poor Centenier died from his wound next day and his murderess was banished from the island

for life.

There is a short cut from the cemetery into Roseville Street, where there is, to the left, both a post office and a chemist. A walk north up Roseville Street leads to La Colomberie, at the eastern end of which is the famous **Howard Davis Park** (St Saviour), while a walk south, down Roseville Street, passing houses with interesting features such as towers, wrought iron balconies, Victorian paving tiles and typically Jersey dormer windows with decorated barge boards, leads directly to the Havre des Pas Swimming Pool and the sea.

A couple of interesting architectural details to notice on the way down into the centre of town are both on the right. The first is the exuberant woodwork on the house called St Ives, which sets off the textured granite so splendidly. Both the stained glass and the gold lettering over the front door are typical of the Victorian period when it was built. Further down the road, opposite the end of Grenville Street, where there is now one of Jersey's Finance Houses, the early nineteeth-century Colomberie House used to stand. It was originally the home of the Hemery family, distant ancestors of the athlete David Hemery, and then housed the Jersey High School for Girls, the Girls' Collegiate School and, lastly, Colomberie House School.

An alternative to turning north from Green Street car park is to turn south and walk down Green Street itself towards the sea. On the right is Jersey's first tunnel road, a continuation of La Route du Fort giving easy access from the south-east to the south-west of the island. Work on the short tunnel, which goes from Green Street to the

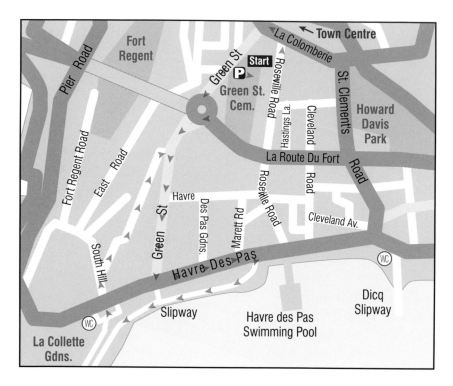

Weighbridge and the harbour area, was completed in 1970.

Further down the road, after the tunnel and opposite the small row of shops known as Clos des Pas, is a stone commemorating the chapel on the south-eastern slope of Le Mont de la Ville which could have given the area of **Havre des Pas** its name, as it was called La Chapelle de Notre Dame des Pas. Now whether this twelfth-century chapel, demolished in 1814 lest it should give cover to an enemy attacking Fort Regent, was dedicated to our Lady of the Footsteps or Our Lady of Peace is a moot point. Certainly tradition has it that Our Lady appeared near the bottom of Green Street and left her footprints on a rock there, but the small harbour that the bay affords would also have been a peaceful one, after negotiating the fearsome rocks that strew its entrance. Whatever its origin, that part of the coastline to the left of Green Street is called Havre des Pas.

Right on the corner, turning left, is a public house whose architectural details, including the two dormer windows, are made the most of by its exterior decoration. Next door is a row of typical fishermen's cottages, dating back to the time before 1824 when Havre des Pas was still a tiny village. After 1824, when a regular steamboat ferry was started between England and Jersey, the elegant Regency houses, which give such period charm to the north side of the coast road to St Clement, were built to accommodate the visitors who began to flock to the island. Particularly attractive are their finely decorated balconies.

Further on are two buildings which exhibit more Victorian features. The hotel on the north side of the road owes much to the Gothic revival, with the pinks of the granite emphasised by the black bands of smooth and textured stone, before the stucco facing of the main part. There are two contrasting types of balcony, the first in wood and the second in iron. During the Occupation this hotel was requisitioned by the Germans. On the sea side of the road opposite is a villa-type building with a tower, having oval dormers looking through its fish-scale slates, which also has distinctive balconies.

After a stroll round the corner to read the plaque commemorating the rock at the Dicq just in St Saviour, where Victor Hugo and other political refugees met to put the world to rights, retrace your footsteps back along the seafront – a delightful example of a Victorian promenade, complete with the original iron railings.

On the seafront here is Jersey's only pretence at a pier, leading to the newly restored Havre des Pas Swimming Pool, where both the large pool and the toddlers' pool are filled with sea water. Inside the rotunda, ice creams and light refreshments can be had and there is also information about the history of the

Havre des Pas Beach

The beach along *Havre des Pas* is popular both with town residents and visitors from nearby hotels and guest houses but it never becomes overcrowded. Bathing is quite safe and is even possible, for those who do not mind a long trek across the sand, at low tide. The strange rock formations which are a feature of this bay afford opportunities for both rock climbing – the Three Sister rocks stretching out to sea are a favourite clamber – and low water fishing, but be careful not to be caught by an incoming tide. At high tide anglers fish from Green Street slipway and supplies of bait etc can be bought from JFS Sport, 4 Clos des Pas, Green Street, St Helier. ☎ 758195.

pool as well as of the Havre des Pas area. From the end of May to 1 October, from 10 am–6 pm every day, a life guard is on duty here and another at West Park's Swimming Pool.

A little further on, the promenade leaves the road to follow the coast. As it does so, it passes where, in the eighteenth-century, a guard house was built by Major General James d'Auvergne to keep a look out for a possible French invasion.

A few steps west beyond this used to be the site of one of the many south coast shipyards that carried on Jersey's profitable shipbuilding in the nineteenth-century. If you look over the railing down at the sea wall, just in front of where the yard was, you will notice that the slipway that used to be there to launch the ships has been filled in with much smaller stones than those in the rest of the wall. A typical journey for one of these Jersey-built ships would have been to Newfoundland to fish for cod.

At Green Street slipway, as well as noting the finely cut granite paving stones and border of the slipway itself, you will see three interesting houses across the road. A little way up Mount Bingham is the imposing villa, Seaview, on whose side wall a prow-shaped window has been added to take every advantage of the sun. A few steps further down is Bramerton House, where Lawrence of Arabia stayed when he was a boy and, no doubt, played on the beach of Havre des Pas. Next door is Du Heaume House where, 40 years earlier, Victor Hugo, during his exile in Jersey, kept his mistress, Juliette Drouet.

Still following the line of the beach west along the promenade, you come

to La Collette. The tower which dominates the skyline ahead – behind the nineteenth-century barracks – is part of Jersey Electricity's power station, while the squat tower to its south is a pre-1830 defence tower, which the Germans adapted in 1944 so that two anti-aircraft guns could be mounted on its top.

To return to Green Street car park, cut up through La Collette Gardens, cross Mount Bingham and walk up South Hill past the gym. Then follow the road as it forks down to the right to Rope Walk, where in the island's shipbuilding days, long twists of hemp were laid out to make ships' ropes. Continue north along Rope Walk, past the Cheshire Home – which often has handmade items for sale – through a small turning to the right and back into Green Street, where several yards ahead on the right, is the multi-storey car park.

2 Pier Road Car Park To The Royal Square And Halkett Place

Leave the car at Pier Road car park, and walk downhill to the crossroads. Turn right past church railings, and continue along Hill Street, noted for the number of lawyers practising there. Turn left at the lights, and on the left across the road is the **Royal Square**. This is a place so packed with memories of the past that a little time should be spent exploring it.

To begin with, this is where the original market in St Helier was always held from the Middle Ages down to the nineteenth-century. The market cross was destroyed at the Reformation but is thought to have stood where the statue of George II is now. From its foot were proclaimed all new laws and public announcements and in the market square itself many criminals, including alleged witches, were pilloried or put to death.

The public buildings round the old market place were only built gradually. The present **Royal Court** – the island's court of justice – is about the fourth replacement of the original cohue, as the courthouse was then called, and was completed in 1866. The arms of George II, from the former building of 1760, are above the public entrance. Inside, the Bailiff's chair with its heraldic carvings dates back to as early as the turn of the sixteenth-century. The Lieutenant-Governor's chair which sits beside it is of a slightly later date. The silver gilt mace, which is always laid before the Bailiff both in court and in the States, was presented by Charles II to the island in recognition of the fact that twice he had found safety there. Its inscription reads 'Not all doth he deem worthy of such a reward'.

The oil paintings which line the walls include portraits of George III and General Conway, the latter by Gainsborough, and a copy of the famous *The Death of Major Peirson* by Copley, the original of which hangs in the Tate Gallery. Once a year, at the beginning of the Michaelmas Law Term, the Seigneurs of the island's fiefs swear allegiance to the Queen, and Royal Court Advocates reaffirm their oaths in the presence of the Bailiff. This sitting of the Assize d'Héritage, thought to be the oldest surviving court in Europe, is preceded by a ceremonial inspection of the Guard of Honour by the Lieutenant-Governor and is followed by a service at the Town Church.

To the east of the Royal Court, with its main distinctively decorated entrance in Halkett Place, is Jersey's seat of government – the island's legislative body – the **States Chamber**, which was built in 1887. Inside, the banner, which is above the Bailiff's chair, is of three leopards passant which feature on the Bailiff's official seal as well as in the heraldic arms of the Queen. There is a gallery in the States Chamber from which visitors may watch and listen to States proceedings every second Tuesday when the House is in session. The other Royal Square buildings house the island records.

Three events worthy of note took place in the Royal Square in the eighteenth-century. The first of these was in 1751 when, to the deafening roar of cannon, the gilded statue of George II – still in the square today – was unveiled. The king is dressed as a Roman senator and rumour at the time had it that the statue was none other than a looted Roman emperor from a Spanish ship

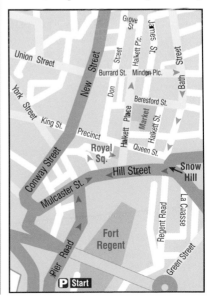

that the local hotelier, who presented the gift to St Helier, had got at a bargain price from a sea captain! This tale, though, does not take into account the fact that the supposed Roman emperor happens to be wearing the Order of the Garter, a distinction unknown to the Romans. Whoever the spindle-shanked statue really represents, it was erected in gratitude for the £300 given by the monarch towards the building of the harbour. The Market Place was renamed in honour of George II and his statue as the Royal Square.

The most dramatic, and finally tragic, episode of the island's history that took place in the Royal Square was the Battle of Jersey. At the beginning of 1781 the French adventurer Baron de Rullecourt, as is mentioned in the history of Grouville, invaded Jersey at La Rocque and marched unchallenged through the night until he reached St Helier. Here de Rullecourt bluffed the Governor Moses Corbet into surrendering the island and all might have been lost for Jersey, if the British forces and the Jersey militia under the command of the young English officer Major Peirson had not disobeyed Corbet's command to surrender too.

Major Peirson swept down from Westmount and through the streets of St Helier in two columns and blocked de Rullecourt and his forces in the Royal Square. Shot marks from the ensuing battle can still be seen on the walls of the public house at the corner of Peirson Place. Sadly, just as the French were being routed from their position in the Square, Major Peirson was fatally wounded and did not live to see the final victory. Baron de Rullecourt also died from wounds

Above: Shopping in St Helier.

Opposite page: St Helier's illumintaed shopping precinct during La Fete de Noue.

Central Market.

The Peirson, Royal Square.

sustained in the fierce fighting and now both victor and vanquished lie at rest in the town church opposite the scene of the Battle of Jersey, which Copley has depicted so dramatically in his painting *The Death of Major Peirson*. A stone commemorating the event is on the ground in the centre of the Royal Square.

Six years after the Battle of Jersey had been fought and won, John Wesley paid an 8-day visit to Jersey during his tour of the Channel Islands. The room in St Helier in which the 81-year-old founder of Methodism preached in 1787 was a privately owned hall above the corn market at the west end of the Royal Square. The corn market is now the Registrar's Office and above it, where Wesley spoke to his Jersey followers, is the United Club.

The visitor will see also, at his or her feet, carved on the paving stones, 'Vega + 1945', now suitably bordered by a black band of stone that was unveiled by HRH The Duchess of Kent in 1985, 40 years after it had been written. The *Vega* was a Swedish ship, sent by the Red Cross, loaded with food parcels and medical supplies for the island's starving inhabitants in the last months of the Occupation. So deeply grateful for the visits of this mercy ship were the islanders, that not only was one baby (born in 1945) actually christened after the Swedish ship but more permanently – underneath the very noses of the occupying German forces – what was forever etched into their memories was set in stone in the Royal Square – V for Vega but also for Victory.

Liberation

The final end of the Occupation is still remembered by those who crammed into the Royal Square on Tuesday 8 May 1945, to hear the Bailiff, later Lord Coutanche, tell them from the balcony over the Royal Court that shortly there was to be a broadcast from England, relayed to them through the huge loudspeakers hoisted in the trees. Then the crowds heard the well-known voice of Winston Churchill proclaim that the war in Europe had just ended and that later that day 'our dear Channel Islands' were to be freed. In fact Jersey was not liberated by British troops until the following day, 9 May, and it is fitting that on every anniversary of that Liberation Day, which is always kept as a public holiday, a service of thanksgiving is held in the Royal Square where the joyful news was first announced. There is a plaque beneath the balcony to tell of that historic occasion in May 1945.

The Royal Square is no longer quite the focal point of island life that it once was but, besides the many stories of the past it has to tell, it is also the venue for several special events. In May and September one of the local artists' guilds holds outdoor exhibitions here; this is where the Variety Club of Jersey set up their annual Town Fayre; and, most appropriately, where the 'Vier Marchi' the old market, with stall-holders in their traditional Jersey sunbonnets is still held during Battle of Britain week in September. In between these special events, there are always the seats under the chestnut trees to sit on and contemplate the amount of history crammed into such a small place.

Leaving the Royal Square by its south-east entrance, opposite the side of the States Chamber, is the office of the Jersey Chamber of Commerce, the first, in 1768, to be founded in the English-speaking world. Turn left and you have a view of the whole width and length of Halkett Place. Look at the wall to the right on which the street's name is placed and you will see how rich it is in architectural motifs, complete with grotesque faces carved on top of the window columns.

Further down on the right is the **Central Market**, which was finally banished from the Royal Square in 1800. This perfect example of a Victorian cast iron market hall is a great favourite with visitors who enjoy its rich architectural detail: noting the gates at the Hilgrove Street and Market Street entrances decorated with the fruit, vegetables and poultry on sale inside; and the much photographed central fountain as well as the fresh wares piled up on the stalls to tempt them. It was opened in 1882 and, despite the food shortage during the Occupation, has been trading ever since in meat, bread, fruit, vegetables and flowers. The smaller fish market is opposite the north side of the large market, in Beresford Street, and visitors will be amazed at the variety of fish it has on offer. There is everything here from dried salted cod, a favourite with old Jersey families and the Portuguese population alike, to conger eel for the

traditional Jersey dish of conger soup, as well as all the shellfish, including the popular spider crab, and other fish, such as mackerel, caught in local waters.

Further down Halkett Place, on the left, is the ornately decorated Mechanics Institute, next to the Central Library, opened by the Queen in 1989. Across the end of the street is the eye-catching Methodist church, known as **Wesley Grove**, with its mixture of classical and Gothic detail. Originally seating 1,600 worshippers, this huge building was first opened in 1847 and now seats about 1,000. It is, therefore, the ideal venue for the concerts of religious music usually given at Christmas and Easter by local and visiting musicians and singers. From Halkett Place the visitor can turn left, left again and right, bringing him into New Street. Turn left, and left again into Burrard Street, and then along Minden Place where out-of-the-way shops can be found.

At the traffic lights, turn right into Bath Street, and walk up the pedestrian precinct. At the top of Bath Street, turn left and immediately right up Snow Hill.

The origin of the small plot of open ground on the far side of the road opposite Snow Hill was that it was the town railway station until 1929, for the Jersey Eastern Railway, and turntable.

Walk on down Hill Street, and turn left at the crossroads uphill to the Pier Road car park.

3 Pier Road Car Park To The Museum, Town Church And Mount Bingham

Leave the car at Pier Road car park, and walk downhill. On the left, at Number 7 Pier Road, is the Société Jersiaise, a

Statue of George II, Royal Square.

look at the outside walls will show the different developments that have taken place in the subsequent centuries. So the walls of the chancel – originally a small chancery chapel – are made of rough boulders brought up from the beach, while local granite squares were used in the fifteenth-century to add the south aisle and south chancel.

At the foot of the pulpit is the memorial that everyone wants to see – given by the States of Jersey to the hero of the Battle of Jersey, Major Peirson. A granite stone in the churchyard marks the grave of his adversary, Baron de Rullecourt.

During the Occupation of Jersey the Town Church was also used by the German troops. Services were conducted by their own chaplains, using their own altar ornaments and the soldiers attending them were

Jersey Society whose members study island subjects, ranging from its antiquities to its original Norman language. Its library is often used by visitors wishing to research either the island's past or – if they have Jersey connections – their own family tree.

Number 7 Pier Road was originally the substantial house of a wealthy merchant, and many of the rooms are now part of the museum, decorated in their original style.

Follow Pier Road down to the crossroads. Facing the visitor on the opposite diagonal are the railings of the oldest building in the town, the **parish church of St Helier**, usually simply called the 'Town Church'. There has been a place of worship on its site at least since the eleventh-century and a

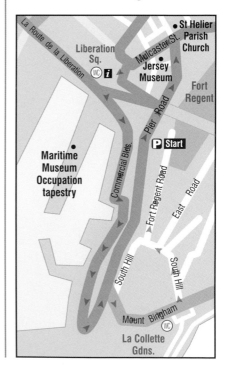

always well behaved. As the Occupation diarist Leslie Sinel commented: 'They left quietly and we went in quietly, for it surely must have been patent to many in the two distinct congregations that we were all worshipping the same God!'

Opposite the north entrance of the church is St Helier's **Church House**, completed in 1970 on the site of the former rectory garden. Its façade is of very pale grey granite quarried at L'Etacq, demonstrating that Jersey's distinctive stone is still being utilised, even if its cost nowadays prohibits more than a mainly decorative use. Church House is often the venue for charity sales, coffees, lunches and teas, so it might be worthwhile for visitors who would enjoy light refreshments served by friendly helpers to call in to see if there is anything on there during their stay.

For the visitor who still has energy, there is a pleasant walk back to Pier Road car park round the harbour and the west flank of Fort Regent. From the Town Church walk down Mulcaster Street to the Weighbridge: ahead is the harbour, to the right across the road is the Tourist Information Centre and just 50yd (46m) round the corner on the Esplanade, well worth deviating from your route for, is the **Island Fortress Occupation Museum**. This exhibition, for which there is an admission charge, features uniformed dummies and various pieces of equipment from World War II. So that the visitor can understand the full implications of all that is on show, including guns, vehicles and authentic documents, there is a video cinema where a clear explanation of Occupation events is shown.

From the **Weighbridge**, notice the decorative architecture of some of the buildings which flank it, in particular the Southampton Hotel, the only Victorian building which remains just as it used to be, down to the detail of its trefoil balustrades, when first built in 1899. The area of the Weighbridge in front of the entrance to the Tourism office was re-christened in May 1995 as 'Liberation Square', to mark the 50th anniversary of the Liberation from German Occupation in May 1945. For this anniversary, a new fountain was constructed, which illustrates the theme of 'liberation' through the group of islanders depicted waving a flag. The fountain was unveiled by the Prince of Wales in the course of his official visit to the island for the anniversary.

Cross the main road at the traffic lights towards the harbour front. Signs

Liberation Square.

will point the visitor to the **Occupation Tapestry Gallery**. This houses the Occupation Tapestry. Each of the twelve Island parishes stitched one panel of this tapestry, which depicts life under the German Occupation.

In the same area of the harbour front are signs to Jersey's **Maritime Museum**. Here visitors will find plenty of nautical exhibits, some simply to look at, others ready for action. Walk back across Liberation Square past the fountain, and you will see ahead of you the **Jersey Museum.**

Once inside you will realise why the Guild of Travel Writers voted it 'The most outstanding tourist attraction in the British Isles'. It has received the National Heritage/IBM 'Museum of the Year' award, while its restaurant won the Gulbenkian 'Best Museum Restaurant of the Year' award.

Starting on the ground floor you should go straight to the Audio Visual Theatre to enjoy a 12-minute 'Jersey – a Place in History' video to get a brief outline of what exactly Jersey was and now is. A simultaneous French translation is available through headphones. Then there is an information station, testing local knowledge for two minutes at a time, which always has a huddle of excited youngsters round it.

What also catches everyone's attention on this floor is the imaginative reconstruction of an Ice Age hunting scene. Here is a craggy rock face down which are climbing some ragged-looking hunters to where their dinner awaits them below.

On the next floor up you will find out how they came to be so lucky in their day's hunting. Here are the mammoths and woolly rhinos that the hunters managed to manoeuvre – perhaps by the strategic use of fire – over the edge of the cliff to their deaths at the bottom. Some of the bones found at the Ice Age site of La Cotte at St Brelade have been placed in position at the base of the reconstructed cliff, just as the archaeologists would have found them.

The whole of the museum's first floor is, in fact, devoted to the 'Story of Jersey'. As well as these 250,000-year-old bones and several artefacts, there are different displays dealing with the island's earliest industries of fishing and farming, Jersey's special relationship with the Crown, archive film, old photographs and, of course, there are several displays dealing with the island's military history, including the Occupation. On the second floor is the Barreau-Le Maistre Art Gallery where, from an art collection of 4,000 items – mainly paintings, prints and drawings by local artists or depicting Jersey subjects – a changing exhibition is held.

The final floor gives a link with two important examples of Jersey's past. The first is the viewing window through which can be seen one of the first signal stations in the British Isles, with a guide to what the flags flying by Fort Regent actually mean. The door next to the viewing window leads into the merchant's house built just after the Napoleonic War. The top three floors have now been restored to how they may have looked in the early 1860s, complete with gas lighting. For children there is also a splendid doll's house on this top floor, made in 1914.

The Museum is open daily and no admission charge needs to be paid to visit the fully-licensed café for tea, coffee, lunch or a snack, or the gift shop, featuring a wide range of local books.

As well as the Jersey Museum and the Jersey Archive, the Jersey Heritage Trust manages five sites through-out the island, which, perhaps more than anything else, can give a visitor an outline of the island's story. These are the Maritime Museum (on the same site as the Occupation Tapestry Gallery), Elizabeth Castle in St Helier, Mont Orgueil Castle (St Martin), Hamptonne Country Life Museum (St Lawrence) and La Hougue Bie (Grouville). Special discount tickets are available which allow entry to any three of the six sites.

On the summit of Town Hill behind the bus terminus can be seen the Lieutenant-Governor's personal standard and the flags fluttering from Great Britain's oldest signal station. Walk round the south of the bus terminus and then cross over by the entrance to the tunnel to Commercial Buildings which runs along the side of the old harbour, across which a glimpse of the ferries from England and France can often be seen. Follow the road round the corner till it comes to the huge wall which separates Commercial Buildings from Pier Road above, opposite Le Quai des Marchands. As the plaque on the wall explains, this wall is 1,000ft (305m) high, was built in 1820 and there are over thirty steps to take you up to Pier Road. If you ignore the steps up and continue along the road past the many openings in the wall on the left, for tools and oakum used in the adjacent shipyards, also on the left you will see on **Mount Bingham** two memorials, one to an Englishman and the other to a Jerseyman, both lost at sea over a hundred years ago.

For a spectacular, panoramic view of the harbour the visitor should follow Mount Bingham – named after a popular former Lieutenant-Governor – round the bend to the left and on and up round the next bend to the right and then look back down at the busy scene below. Here there are attractive terraced grounds and a children's playground.

At the top of Mount Bingham **La Collette Gardens** are beautifully laid out – a green oasis with the sea on three sides – in memory of one of Jersey's benefactors, Benjamin Meaker. Here, apart from the spring and summer bedding plants, the observant visitor will discover the sweet scented violets and the buds of pink japonica in spring and the cascades of mesembryanthemums in summer. Look east and there through the trees is the bay which stretches from Havre des Pas across to Grève d'Azette. Ahead, to the far south, is Icho Tower and Green Island and, further north, the four modern tower blocks, one of twentieth-century Jersey's architectural mistakes.

After a rest here to admire this view, continue on down Mount Bingham and cross over the road to go up South Hill, which passes behind both the swimming pool and Fort Regent. For the keen explorer of byways, the lane called East Road, that runs south to north just before the swimming pool, follows the ramparts of Fort Regent and leads to the crossroads where Green Street meets the tunnel and continues over the bridge into Regent Road – a pleasantly quiet way into town by way of Colomberie.

From the Glacis field, next to the path which leads up to the back of the swimming pool but which does not give an entrance to it, there is another fine view – this time over the east of the town and up to the Gothic building on the skyline, *Victoria College for Boys*, founded in 1852. This is sometimes the venue for both concerts and cricket matches open to the general public. The first turning after this leads to Fort Regent, where there is a lift down to Pier Road car park; the second road also winds down to Pier Road with the car park to the right.

4 Minden Place To The Jersey Arts Centre And St Thomas' Church

Minden Place was so named in commemoration of the Battle of Minden, fought in Saxony, north Germany, in 1759, which brought an end to the Seven Years War. The plaque in Minden Place also commemorates the part played in that battle by the Royal Hampshire Regiment, the King's Own Scottish Borderers and the Royal Artillery, under

Les Petit Train de Jersey

Tourist Trains *Lille* and *Terence* depart opposite the Grand Hotel every 30 minutes between 10am and 5pm and run along the bay to St Aubin. *Major Pierson* departs from Liberation Square every 45 minutes and takes visitors on a historical circular tour of St Helier. Trains do not run outside of the main tourist season. A special ticket can be purchased when boarding any of these trains. The hopper ticket entitles the holder to a trip on all three trains.

*Above: Maritime Museum and
Tapestry Gallery.*

Right. Steam Clock.

Jersey Museum.

the command of the Jerseyman Captain Charles Le Geyt, who later became the island's first postmaster.

Leaving Minden Place car park, walk east towards Bath Street and cross the road into Phillips Street, where a little way down on the left is the **Jersey Arts Centre**. Opened in 1982, the complex includes a theatre, a gallery, a bar and a restaurant. The Benjamin Meaker Theatre was the last part of the Centre to be completed and is a compact venue for plays and concerts, from classical to folk and jazz, seating 250. In the Berni Gallery on the first floor regular exhibitions are shown of both local and international artists, which can usually be viewed by visitors without an admission charge.

On the ground floor are the rooms where various courses in dance and crafts take place, as well as the well- appointed bar and restaurant. This is a favourite place for local people to relax over a drink or a meal and visitors are welcome too. Pre-theatre suppers or suppers after the show are also available, but it is advisable to book these in advance.

There are special provisions in the Arts Centre for the disabled, as wheelchairs can come through the main entrance on the ground floor, where the toilets are also situated. Advance notice, or arrival half an hour before the performance starts, however, is advisable for anyone in a wheelchair who wants to go to the Benjamin Meaker Theatre. For the hard of hearing, there is a hearing loop throughout the theatre. Contact the box office for further information.

Leaving the Arts Centre, turn left into Providence Street, where one comes across a small modern town housing estate which must be second to none for the number of keen gardeners who make the most of every inch of their tiny gardens. From Providence Street turn right into Charles Street, and straight on into Bath Street. To the left, at the junction of Bath Street, Beresford Street and Peter Street, is **West's Centre**. Here, under the shade of young trees, one can sit and watch the world go by. West's Centre is sometimes the venue for the Jersey Art Exhibitors' Guild to display a selection of local art.

After a rest in West's Centre, walk a little further up the precinct into Hilgrove Street, which used to be known as French Lane, because French farm workers used to congregate here on a Saturday afternoon. To the right is Halkett Place, but if you take the left turning into Hilgrove Street and then the first turning to the left again into Hilary Street, the square has been made with Peter Street and one is ready to walk north up Bath Street. As you walk, note the fine top half of many of the buildings: such as the one at the corner of Charles Street on the east side of the road and the French-style roof on the corner of Minden Place opposite. Continue walking up Bath Street, which becomes David Place, until the crossroads with Victoria Street and Stopford Road. On the right is the Royal Hotel, fronted by its elegant standard roses.

At the bottom of Victoria Street is the Catholic **church of St Thomas**, built in 1887 in the style of the thirteenth-century. This is the largest Roman Catholic church in the Channel Islands.

From St Thomas' church, turn south down Val Plaisant which becomes **New Street**. This hotch-potch of a road was, in the eighteenth-century, mainly

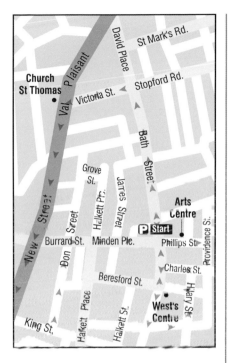

St Paul's church which was built in the Gothic revival style popular in 1891. Visitors are welcome to the services at St Paul's.

Opposite St Paul's, notice the fine side entrance to de Gruchy's which was opened by the merchant Abraham de Gruchy in 1826. In 1854 the store was thought comparable 'to the best in London' Its founder died in 1864 and was buried in Green Street cemetery and the store is no longer owned by the family.

Mr Voisin

Next door to the church is Voisins, the family firm that was begun as a tiny back street shop in 1837 by François Voisin. That it grew to its present-day proportions is largely due to the fact that Mr Voisin left the selling to his assistants and gave his own personal attention to the buying of goods for his shop to sell. In his diary he records his journeys all over Europe, as well as his regular visits to the great fur fair in Russia and his search in the East for silks and damask.

gardens, where the townsfolk used to grow their vegetables when their day's work was over. It was laid in the nineteenth-century to join Val Plaisant in the north to La Rue de Derrière in the south which is now known as King Street. The pharmacy at the junction with Devonshire Place has been dispensing drugs since that time, as the sign outside shows, though it no longer includes the painless extraction of teeth among its services!

Another building with an interesting history began life as a chapel, before becoming the Playhouse theatre, then a carpet shop, and now houses luxury apartments.

On the east side of the street, are two more nineteenth-century buildings: the former Trustee Savings Bank built in 1870, now with a 1987 extension, and

To get back to Minden Place car park, walk up King Street as far as Don Street, turn left and walk past the pavement cafés and on to the junction of Don Street and Burrard Street. Turn right here and the multi-storey car park is on your left, opposite the rear entrance to the fish market.

Other Places of Interest in the Parish

There is more to the parish of St Helier, though, than the town. Incredible as it may seem, there are still farms and smallholdings with a St Helier address, so anyone who wants to sample the countryside of the parish should go north up Val Plaisant and Trinity Road (A8) and then turn left into **La Vallée des Vaux**. Here there is a tranquil walk past the water meadows, where the cows graze, the brooks and gardens and a pond where local children come to feed the ducks.

A circular walk back into St Helier can be taken by walking up the stone steps about halfway along La Vallée des Vaux on the left, going along the narrow footpath called Highfield Lane and then turning left into La Pouquelaye. On the way you pass the UK's smallest independent television station, Jersey's Channel Television which goes out on Channel 3. La Pouquelaye is another pleasant walk, though more built up, which takes its name from the fact that a menhir – a fairy stone or *pouquelaye* – stands in a nearby farm. This menhir, though, is on private property and access is not given to the general public to view it.

Walk down La Pouquelaye, past the D'Auvergne playing fields and Almorah cemetery on the left, and pass by the side of **Almorah Crescent**. Take a moment to look through the gateway, for this crescent of ten houses, though built between 1845–50, is probably the most distinguished example of Regency architecture not just in Jersey but in the whole of the Channel Islands. From its commanding position its distinctive design can be picked out across the plateau of the town from as far away as Elizabeth Castle. The name Almorah for both the crescent and the cemetery behind it comes from the fact that the wife of the speculative builder who put up the crescent was born in Almorah in the Himalayas.

The walker can get into town by walking across the front of the crescent and down – taking the furthest one of the pair of steps that lead up to the crescent – into Upper Midvale Road. By following Midvale Road into Bath Street, one is back in the centre of town. The car driver continues down La Pouquelaye and turns left into Queen's Road, past one of Jersey's most interesting Victorian properties, Le Chalet, on the left. The three-house terrace is wholly built of

Mappin & Webb, Queen Street.

Battle of Flowers Parade, St Helier.

granite – the shaping and placing of the blocks is outstanding – and has some of the most spectacular timber fretwork, originally done by hand, on the island.

Another way into the less urban parts of St Helier is to go north up St John's Road. On the way up on the right are the display beds with their contrasting colours of both St Helier's and the State's nurseries, from whence come the plants to beautify the public parks and gardens in St Helier and the rest of the island. For walkers or drivers who want to deviate from the main road there is one way to the right and one to the left before the nurseries to get off it and into the country.

Turn right down La Rue des Côtils and one comes into La Vallée des Vaux with its gorse-covered *côtils* from its northern end. Turn left down La Verte Chemin, and you come to the steep hill of La Rue de Moulin du Fliquet at the bottom of which is **Bellozanne Valley**. This valley, which comes down to the sea at First Tower, got its name from a monastery in Normandy called Bellozanne Abbey, to which King John of England gave the Jersey valley as a gift. It remained in the control of the Normandy abbey until the time of Henry V and was therefore known as Bellozanne Valley, with the hill behind it being called **Mont à l'Abbé**.

Where Bellozanne comes into the St Aubin's Inner Road, to the left is the animal cemetery and to the right is a Neolithic burial mound.

To the right, at **First Tower** (La Première Tour), named after the first in a series of defensive towers in St Aubin's Bay, built around 1790, is **First Tower Park**. In the park, side by side,

are examples of both pagan and Christian belief and ritual. In the centre of the park, under a grove of trees, is both a gallery grave and a cistin-circle. The gallery grave, dating from about 2500BC, is similar to the one described at Le Couperon but, unusually, it was reused around 1800BC for a Beaker culture burial. The stones it is built of are of L'Islet (where Elizabeth Castle now is) granite and, though it contained no bones, twenty-two beakers, some Jersey bowls and an archer's wrist-guard were found. The monument itself remained undiscovered, however, for thousands of years, as it was not till 1869 that its existence was suspected and excavations finally began.

To the east of Ville ès Nouaux, as this dolmen is called, stands the Anglican church of St Andrew, also built in granite. It took its name from a small seaman's chapel built on the Esplanade in 1850 to serve not just the busy port, but also the shipbuilding industry which flourished then. When this came to an end, the chapel was closed down and its name and endowments given to the new church, urgently needed to serve the fast-growing community to the west of the parish.

In First Tower Park, or St Andrew's Park, as it is also called, there is a children's playground and plenty of space for sitting or walking, with the sea and the beach just across two roads.

The best way to explore these outskirts of St Helier is, of course, on a bike. There are many places in town where cycles can be hired at a modest cost, by the day or week as preferred. There is also 'Le Petit Train de Jersey' (see box on p46).

Places to Visit

Elizabeth Castle

L'Islet, St Aubin's Bay, St Helier

☎ 01534 723971

www.jerseyheritage.org

Open: daily 1st April to 31st Oct 10am–6pm. Reduced admission charge for senior citizens and students; children under 6 free. Limited access for those with mobility impairment.

Island Fortress Occupation Museum

9 Esplanade,

St Helier

☎ 01534 734300

Open: Mar to Apr 9.30am–6.30pm; May to Sep 9.30am–9.30pm; Oct to Feb 10am–4pm; Admission charge.

Jersey Animal Cemetery

First Tower

St Helier

☎ 01534 724331

Jersey Museum & Art Gallery

The Weighbridge, St Helier
☎ 01534 633300

www.jerseyheritage.org

Open: daily all year round. 9.30am – 5pm. Reduced admission charge for senior citizens and students; children under 6 free.

Maritime Museum and Occupation Tapestry Gallery

New North Quay,

St Helier,

☎ 01534 811043

www.jerseyheritage.org

Open: daily summer 10am–5pm, winter 10am–4pm. Reduced admission charge for senior citizens and students; children under 6 free.

The Royal Court

Royal Square, St Helier

Public entrance to Public Gallery when court sits Mon–Fri, starts 10am. Not otherwise open.

States Chambers

Royal Square, St Helier

Public entrance to Public Gallery when States sit on alternate Tuesdays, starting at 9.30am. Not otherwise open.

Town Hall

York Street, St Helier

☎ 01534 811811

Not open to public, but anyone wishing to view pictures in Assembly Room, go to reception.

2. St Saviour, St Clement and Grouville

Around St Saviour

Once a predominantly agricultural parish, the western tip of St Saviour has become increasingly built up, serving as a kind of suburb to St Helier. The heart of this long narrow parish to the north-east of town is round the church, with the Parish Hall, built in 1890, opposite and the lane running south by the side of it leading to Government House. This spot is also the focal point for tourists visiting the parish, as it was in St Saviour's Rectory that the famous Edwardian beauty Lillie Langtry was born; in St Saviour's Church that she was twice married; and in its graveyard that she was buried.

The full name of one of the four chapels which eventually became St Saviour's church (*Bus 3b*) – St Saviour of the Thorn – tells of an old Christian belief. During the time when the whole of Europe was Catholic, no altar could be consecrated unless it contained a holy relic. So it is thought that the owner of the original small thatched chapel had in it either a thorn from Christ's crown of thorns, or a thorn from the sacred Glastonbury thorn planted by Joseph of Arimathea. This thorn is still remembered in the parish crest of three nails surrounded by a crown of thorns.

The church that eventually sprang in the twelfth-century from this, St Sauveur de l'Epine, together with the three other private chapels, is well worth a visit and not just because Lillie Langtry was married and buried there.

Outside the church there are three items of note: on the south-west corner, set into a buttress, is a scallop shell, probably commemorating a pilgrimage from St Saviour to the shrine of St James in Compostela; there are several medieval windows, including two with flamboyant tracery on the eastern wall; at this eastern end are two megalithic blocks which could have come from an earlier church, or even a pagan place of worship.

Inside, the church, with its two chancels and two naves side by side, is rather dark because of the stained glass in every window, but there are time switches for the visitor to use. With the lights on, the glory of the chancel window, dating back to the 1440s, with the dignity of its simple lines, and the more modern colours of the fine pre-Raphaelite stained glass can be enjoyed to the full.

On the south wall of the south nave is a memorial to Canon Cohu, who acted as the rector of the parish during the Occupation. He was imprisoned by the Germans for spreading British news from the BBC heard on a hidden wireless. He was later sent away to a concentration camp in Germany, where he died.

A more recent addition to the Lady Chapel is a replica of a cannon taken from one of the parish's Battle of Flowers floats. This symbolises the real cannon which stood here, until about 200 years ago, as in most island parish churches. The Armoury Meeting Room, which stands behind the church, was once the gunpowder store.

On the north wall are memorials to the relations of Lillie Langtry – the Le Breton family. The impressive oak carving in the church and the painting of the reredos panel were by Jerseymen.

In that part of the cemetery known as Le Clos de l'Hotel Dieu is the grave, clearly signposted, that everyone comes to see – where the Jersey lily, Lillie Langtry was buried. The purity and delicacy of her monument – just a few feet away from a widespreading beech – is in striking contrast to the heavy granite memorials in the rest of the churchyard. The two small oaks which stand either side of the lychgate were, incredibly, planted from acorns found in a joint of venison sent to a rector of St Saviour at the end of the last century!

Government House to the south of the church is the official residence of the Queen's representative in the island, the Lieutenant-Governor. The main drive to what was originally an early nineteenth-century merchant's house, built in the French 'pavilion' style, is to the left up the steep hill, overhung with trees, from St Helier to Five Oaks – St Saviour's Hill. Every year an invitation is extended to the people of Jersey to attend the garden party held at Government House on the Queen's official birthday in June. Otherwise the house is not open to the public, though the lodge and glimpses of the house can be seen from the road.

It was in Government House in 1876 that two Edwardian beauties, both born in Jersey, had an unusual meeting. They were the novelist Elinor Glyn and the society beauty Lillie Langtry.

Elinor Glyn (1864-1943) was born Nellie Sutherland and, after an absence of 7 years returned with her mother and stepfather to live in a rented house, 'Richelieu', in St Saviour. The future novelist's reading was only from the library shelves that she could reach, so it included such diverse titles as *Don Quixote* in eighteenth-century French, the *Illustrated History of England* and *Kingsley's Heroes*.

Her impressions of the seas round Jersey were lasting. Of a high spring tide she had witnessed at La Collette, westwards along the coast from the Dicq, she wrote in 1936, 'the awful mountains of water hurling themselves against the jagged rocks there ... the vision of them comes back to me in my nightmares even now.'

When she left Jersey she became the beautiful and intelligent companion of men like Lord Curzon, the author of the banned *Three Weeks*, who had written about her the famous lines:

Would you like to sin
with Elinor Glyn
On a tiger skin?
Or would you prefer
To err
With her on some other fur?

And the meeting between Elinor Glyn and Lillie Langtry took place when Elinor was only 12 and she and her sister and the Lieutenant-Governor's daughter hid under a dressing table in Government House to get a glimpse of the Jersey Lily as she took off her cloak. When a fit of the giggles gave them away, Mrs Langtry promised not to tell on them and even had some supper sent up for them in the nursery.

Emilie Charlotte Le Breton was born in St Saviour's Rectory, just behind the church, the daughter of the Dean of Jersey, on 13 October 1853. Both her parents were known for their good looks and she obviously inherited her beauty from them. However, as a girl she was a tomboy, always hoping to be included in the escapades of her elder brothers. These involved stealing door knockers from houses hearby; scaring parishioners as they walked through the adjacent churchyard and being dared to run down the lane with nothing on!

She was only 14 when she received her first offer of marriage, but was 20 when she met the man who was to take her from Jersey and introduce her to London society. He was Edward Langtry, a rich Belfast widower who was in Jersey as a guest at Lillie's brother's wedding. One of the wedding festivities was a dance given on his 200-ton yacht, *Red Gauntlet*, and it was there that Edward and Lillie met. They were engaged 6 weeks later and

were married in St Saviour's church on 9 March 1874

Lillie caused her first major sensation when she accompanied her husband, 2 years later, to a reception given by a well-known London hostess of that time, Lady Sebright, in Lowndes Square. All the other women present were wearing colourful, elaborate and restricting clothes: Lillie appeared in a plain black, square cut dress, made by a St Helier dressmaker. She had no jewellery and her auburn hair was twisted carelessly into a knot at the nape of her neck. As if her simple style were not enough, those at Lowndes Square that day were also impressed by her beauty and her vivacity.

Lillie was painted in that same black dress by Sir John Millais, who also came from Jersey, when they were both in London The flower she holds in her hand is meant to be a Jersey lily – hence the double meaning of the title Jersey Lily for the title of the portrait – but, as they could not find one in London, they had to make do with a lily from Guernsey! The painting, which caused a sensation when it was exhibited at the Royal Academy in 1878, can be seen in the Barreau-Le Maistre Art Gallery in the Jersey Museum, together with Sir Edward Poynter's *Mrs Langtry*.

Soon after her success at Lady Sebright's, Lillie Langtry was introduced to the Prince of Wales. From that moment her life became an endless whirl of socialising – often in the company of the Prince of Wales. Her husband preferred to go off by himself to a life of fishing and drinking.

For several seasons Lillie's triumph as the Prince of Wales' acknowledged mistress was unallayed, but then society, as suddenly as it had taken her up, dropped her. She remained a friend of the Prince of Wales and his wife to the end, but when she was found to be no longer the pet of society, tradesmen began to press for the payment of the huge bills she had run up. Bailiffs eventually took possession of her London house and Lillie fled back to Jersey.

When she returned to London it was as an actress. She appeared as Kate Hardcastle in *She Stoops to Conquer* at the Haymarket theatre and in other plays. Later there followed a tour of the United States. During her 5-year stay in America several things happened: Lillie begged a divorce from Edward but he refused; she became a naturalised American citizen; and a town in Texas was renamed Langtry in her honour.

On Lillie's return to England she was determined to fight her way back to society – through racing. She started up a racing stable of her own and in 1897 won the Cesarewich with her horse Merman. The Prince of Wales himself publicly escorted her into the Jockey Club enclosure. Forty-eight hours after Merman's victory, which brought her £39,000, she learned of the death of her husband Edward, in Chester Asylum.

Two years later, when she was already 46, Lillie married Sir Hugo Gerald de Bathe, a young guardsman of 28. They were married, as she and Edward had been, in St Saviour's church. Then they bought a small cottage in Beaumont in St Peter, which Lillie insisted should be called 'Merman'.

Lillie's stay in Jersey was not a long one – she felt the call of both London and the stage. Once back there she bought the dilapidated Imperial Theatre in Westminster and spent over £50,000 in restoring it. Her venture was not a success and after World War I she retired from the stage and London and built a villa in Monte Carlo. Lillie died there in 1929 but, as she had specifically requested, her body was brought back to Jersey to be buried in St Saviour's churchyard near the church where she had been baptised and twice married.

Each October there is a special event linking Jersey and Bournemouth, through their association with Lillie Langtry. For it was in Bournemouth that Bertie, the Prince of Wales, built in 1877 a house for his Jersey lily, where they could enjoy their close relationship out of public sight. It was called The Red House and still stands today, a fine building in its own grounds. Now, though, it is a hotel called The Langtry Manor and it is the Bournemouth centre for the double celebration of Lillie Langtry's fame and beauty.

Though the area round the church may be regarded as the centre of the parish for tourists because of its Lillie Langtry associations, the shopping centres are to be found at the top and bottom of the parish. Continuing up St Saviour's Hill after the church is Five Oaks. Here, where St Saviour's Hill, Bagatelle Road, Prince's Tower Road and La Grande Route de St Martin meet, are several shops, including banks (*Bus 3, 3a, 3b, 23*).

Walk a short distance from here down Bagatelle Road, passing St Saviour's Primary School on the right-hand side. A small grassy island at the end of the lane which runs along the south-west side of the school was chosen as the site for the Parish Millennium Cross. Each of the island's 12 parishes has a similar cross.

Not far from the Millennium Cross is a pleasant walk through Swiss Valley. Start from La Rue de la Retraite until it turns first right into La Rue de Beauvoir. On the left are Le Quesne's Nurseries, where you can park your car. Turn left out of the car park and walk down La Rue de Beauvoir as far as the junction with Les Varines. Go down the lane on the left of the archway ahead and turn left into a field. Follow the footpath along the top of the field till you enter a wooded area where the path divides. For an easy walk, turn right here and, after about 10 minutes, you will come to the gardens of the Longueville Manor Hotel. From here you can go back the same way as you came.

Once back at the car park, a relaxing time can be spent looking at the large selection of plants and gifts on display in the shop at the Nurseries.

Down in the south of the parish, in Georgetown, there are more shops, banks and a supermarket with a post office (*Bus 1, 1b*).

Further to the east on the Longueville Road is another parade of shops, which also includes a bank (*Bus 1b*).

Jersey's largest trading estate is also on the Longueville Road where 50 *vergées* were allocated in 1970 for the use of light industry and activities which are better sited out of St Helier. The estate also contains Jersey's new, modern postal headquarters.

Opposite La Rue des Prés Trading Estate is **Longueville Garden Centre** (*Bus 1b*). It is tucked away behind the main road in New York Lane, which is the second turning left after Longueville Manor. This clearly laid-out gardener's paradise is becoming increasingly popular with visitors, because here they can often buy plants they cannot find in the UK. More than that, visitors are appreciative of the fact that the assistants have the time to give tips on the best way to grow the plants they buy. The garden centre has its own car park.

The obvious centre of sporting activities in this parish is the **Grainville Sports Ground** (*Bus 3b*) at the top of St Saviour's Hill to the left, on the way up to Five Oaks. League Cricket is played here every evening during the season and first class matches with visiting teams at weekends. There is ample room for spectators – who can enjoy between overs the view across to the sea or below to the cows grazing in the fields – as they settle themselves comfortably in sun or shade on the banks around the pitch. Charity cricket matches are also held here and attract a great deal of local support.

Anyone with a love of horses will enjoy attending the Jersey Horse Driving Society shows which are held here three times a year, with the spring show in May, the qualifiers' show in June and the members' show in August.

St Saviour's Bowls Club has its headquarters here, but any visitor who wishes to play must be a member of a bowls club back home. Although there are tennis courts beyond the bowling green, these are usually fully booked by schools or clubs. Adjacent to the Grainville sports ground is Jersey's indoor bowling stadium, which is available for use all year round. Holidaymakers can register with the club as day visitors; ☎ 01534 768772 for more information.

During the winter, the spectator sports are football and hockey. There is a sports pavilion with full changing and shower facilities for anyone taking part in any of the sports facilities provided at Grainville and plenty of space for parking.

A long established tennis club, the **Caesarean Tennis Club** (*Bus 21, 23*) can be found on Les Grands Vaux, on the left going north towards Grands Vaux Reservoir. Here there are eight all-weather courts, four of which can be floodlit, plus full club facilities, which include a bar and a snooker room. This is a members' club, but visitors are welcome to come and play or to watch the various tournaments which are put on during the season. The airdrome courts are for members only. ☎ 01534 519177

In the leisure complex of the Hotel de France, the **Lido de France** (*Bus 3b, 21, 23*) in St Saviour's Road, visitors are welcome to join in the weight training, aerobics and squash and other activities, which are available there.

There is a grisly legend connecting St Saviour's only surviving manor, **Longueville Manor** (*Bus 1b, 2c, 22*) and the field which lies next to it. The field was called Le Pré d'Anthoine and the sixteenth-century Seigneur, or Lord of the Manor, Hostes Nicolle, wanted to add this sole possession of a poor butcher to the many *rergées* of land he already owned. Despite being Bailiff of Jersey, Nicolle could think of no legal way of getting Anthoine's property and land for himself, so he got it by trickery, with terrible consequences.

He told two of his servants to kill two of his best sheep and hide them in

Anthoine's house. Next day he told the Constable that two of his sheep were missing and the Constable eventually found them – hanging dead in the butcher's stable. Anthoine was arrested, tried, found guilty and sentenced to death. As the hangman put the noose round his neck, the innocent butcher turned towards Nicolle and said 'I summon you to appear within forty days before the just judge of all to answer for this injustice!' On the thirty-ninth day after Anthoine's execution, Hostes Nicolle fell dead. From that time a curse was put on all the Seigneurs of Longueville Manor that they would never have a male heir and that, when their time came to die, clattering hooves of phantom horses would be heard in the courtyard.

Perhaps the curse has come true because today there is no Seigneur of Longueville, though the coat of arms of the wicked Hostes Nicolle can still be seen on top of the fine stone arch round the front door of his manor. The *colombier* built by a later Seigneur of Longueville – a prestigious status symbol, as well as the source of plentiful pigeon pie – still stands to the north of the manor. Access to it is up La Rue St Thomas and through a gate on the left. The circular *colombier*, or dovecote, is on the right of the path leading from the gate.

The manor is now a five-star hotel, where both locals and visitors like to take advantage of its reputation for good food. Longueville Manor Hotel is on the Longueville Road.

The **Rocher des Proscrits** makes St Saviour's only stretch of coast, near Le Dicq (*Bus 18*) in St Clement's Bay, famous. It was here that Victor Hugo and other political refugees from Europe would discuss their revolutionary plans to put the world to rights. It has a plaque to mark it and is near the Le Dicq slipway. From Le Dicq there is Havre des Pas to the west to explore, with its swimming pool and beaches, in the parish of St Helier, and the long sandy stretch of Grève d'Azette to the east, in the parish of St Clement.

The island's only further education college, **Highlands College** (*Bus 3b, 21,23*), whose entrance for car drivers is along Bon Air Lane, which runs one way from Wellington Road to St Saviour's Hill. Pedestrians should walk up Highland Lane, the first turning to the right after *Hôtel de France*. The original house, which probably dated back to 1800, was bought by the English branch of the Jesuits in 1894, to extend it and turn it into a French naval preparatory school. This school later returned to France and a French secondary school took its place until after World War I. The last religious order to run Highlands as the French Brothers of Christian Education who sold the property to the States of Jersey in 1972. The Brothers stayed at Highlands throughout the Occupation, despite the German Army requisitioning part of the building, and reported that the Germans respected both them and their work, as well as their three chapels.

Anyone who wants to learn about the generous benefactions given to the island in memory of the young Howard Davis who fell in World War I should go to the memorial hall in **Howard Davis Park** to the left of the main gate on the corner of Don Road. Here in the tranquil room is the story of young

Howard told in words and photographs until his untimely death in action near Boulogne in 1916. Outside are the ornamental gardens which his grieving father had laid out as a perpetual memorial to him and which were officially opened in 1939.

Since then, many locals and visitors have looked on this as their favourite park. Immediately in front of the main gate is the statue of George V and behind it the flagstaff which was originally from one of the wealthy Mr Davis' yachts. The beds near the statue depict in hundreds of tiny plants the logos of any organisation celebrating a special anniversary that year.

Further into the park, there is the sweep of a wide and carefully tended lawn, where holidaymakers can lie in the sun or listen to one of the visiting bands and children can dance to the music. To the left of this long lawn are heather beds, a rockery and the peaceful, walled rose garden where over a thousand roses, all clearly labelled and carefully tended, bloom throughout the summer. These 10 acres (4 hectares) of park with their beds of colourful flowers and shrubs are a must for all garden lovers.

The church at the south end of the park also has a strong connection with Mr T. B. Davis, the park's creator. St Luke's church was his family's church, where he himself sang in the choir and it was here he attended, quite by chance, his own memorial service! Running away to sea at 14, Tom Davis was shipwrecked off Norfolk, drifted 36 hours by himself in a small boat in the North Sea, and was finally rescued by a passing boat and brought back to Jersey. When he landed, as it was

Statue of George V in Howard Davis Park.

Samarès Manor.

Samarès Manor.

a Sunday, he went straight to St Luke's church, only to find the vicar holding a memorial service for him!

Davis was soon back at sea, however, and made himself a millionaire, organising coastal traffic along the shores of Africa. After his son Howard had been killed, he set aside part of his great wealth to benefit islanders in his memory. So as well as Howard Davis Park, there is also the theatre at Victoria College, and an experimental farm, as well as various scholarships, bearing his son's name.

To the west of St Luke's church is the **War Cemetery** which was dedicated in 1943 as the last resting place for Allied airmen or sailors who lost their lives while fighting over or around Jersey. On 16 November 1943, for example, many bodies were washed ashore, especially in the west of the island. They were members of the crews of the British ships *Charybdis* and *Limbourne*, who had lost their lives in a naval engagement with the Germans in the Gulf of St Malo on 22 October. To begin with, the twenty bodies were all buried with full naval honours in a common grave at Mont à l'Abbé, but were later reburied in this special cemetery. All the graves are marked by a simple wooden cross and are always part of the island's Remembrance Day services.

St Clement

Around the Parish

Covering the south-east tip of the island, St Clement is not only Jersey's smallest parish but also the most southerly parish in the British Isles. With one of the rockiest coastlines and perhaps the most fertile land, St Clement is also noted for its long stretches of sandy beach, its prehistoric remains, a fine manor house and tales of superstition and witchcraft. It was also, for over 3 years, the home of the famous French writer Victor Hugo. The site where his house once stood is on the coast road. Here, and in the surrounding area, is a ribbon development of luxury apartment blocks. Despite these, and the ugly intrusion of the four high-rise blocks of States flats on the Le Marais skyline, making this small parish the one with the fourth-highest population, St Clement is still in many parts – with its small fields and many hedges – a charming part of the island.

St Clement shares its northern boundaries with St Saviour and Grouville and extends from just west of Plat Rocque Point westwards to Le Dicq (pronounced dyke) slipway. This dyke was one of the first attempts to combat the devastating effects of so much parish land lying below high-tide level. Before it was constructed, much land was lost, as can still be seen when exceptionally low tides lay bare the remnants of a great forest now lying beneath the sands of Grève d'Azette. In 1811 even the dyke was not strong enough to hold back the seas and the extensive flooding that year forced the States to build the high sea wall along this beach.

Looking seaward from this south-eastern corner the view is of fantastically shaped reefs and broken rocks. The lunar-like landscape stretches from the coast to far out to sea with many of the rocky peaks at the ebb and flow of the tide just below the surface of the water – a constant navigational hazard. Yet defence of 'this terrible coast', as it has been called, was still thought necessary at the time when a French invasion was feared. So in 1780 a tower was built at **Le Hocq** and, in 1811, on the rock islet of Icho a quarter of a mile out in St Clement's Bay, a second tower – 28ft (8.5m) high. In the autumn, on nearby reefs, herons can sometimes be seen waiting for the high tide to ebb.

A third tower, a well-known landmark, dating back at least to the eighteenth-century, overlooks the parish and its coastline from a high spur of land to the north-west of La Rue au Blancq. This is known as Nicolle Tower and has been used over the centuries, including the time of the German Occupation, as a look-out station. The Nicolle Tower is now a Landmark Trust property which is let to visitors as holiday accommodation.

Remains of the parish's earliest visitors, from prehistoric times, have been found both on the coast and inland. On the tidal islet 300yd (270m) from the promontory that divides Grève d'Azette and St Clement's Bay, eighteen cist or box-like graves were discovered, some still with human remains. La Motte, or **Green Island** (*Bus 1*) as it is known today, is a grass-covered rock about 200ft (61m) long which is surrounded by water only at high tide. Today it is a favourite picnic spot for local families, being within such easy reach of St Helier, while several of the cist graves have been removed to the museum at La Hougue Bie in Grouville to save them from being washed away by the tide. Much of the island has been lost over recent years by the effects of rain and sea, together with wear and tear from the many people visiting the landmark. Work is being undertaken in an attempt to prevent further erosion.

Samarès

Sir James Knott, who bought the fief of Samarès in 1924, had at one time forty gardeners to carry out his own ambitious plans to drain the marsh so that he could construct unusual rockeries and water gardens as well as a special spot for the subtropical plants he collected. To this garden, the largest in Jersey, he also introduced an oriental theme, with a series of waterfalls, a pagoda and a summerhouse in the Japanese style.

Today many of the garden features introduced by the various Seigneurs of Samarès can still be traced. For instance in the spring there is the magnificent sight of over eighty varieties of camellias in bloom. There are also different corners of the grounds made into specialised areas such as a herb garden, a walled garden and a water rock garden. The herb garden itself is sub-divided too, into four different sections of cosmetic, culinary, fragrant and medicinal herbs. All the herbs are set out and labelled to give visitors easy access to them as well as the pleasure of their distinctive scents.

There is also a herb garden café where you can enjoy morning coffee, lunch or traditional Jersey cream teas. In the farmyard there is a craft centre with spinning and weaving to watch, plus wood-turning and soap-making, as well as an animals corner. There is also a shop selling potpouri and books about herbs and live souvenirs of Jersey in the shape of potted herb plants. The scavenger hunt offers the children an exciting way to discover the manor's secrets and meet some of the animals.

The manor, too, is open to visitors, though, because of successive modernisations, only the thickness of the walls and St Martha's crypt testify to its original antiquity. However, across the drive from the manor's front door stands the island's oldest *colombier* or dovecote, dating back to the eleventh-century, which only Seigneurs were allowed to have. Tradition has it that owls use the Samarès *colombier* as a base when they fly from Longueville Manor in the parish of St Saviour.

Noteworthy features inside the manor include the fine French walnut panelling in the dining room where there is a Simon Elwes portrait of the late Dame of Samarès in riding habit. The drawing room, with its specially woven carpet of sage green and the Steinway piano, in its ornate case after the Dutch style, is often used for concerts given by both local and internationally known musicians. The intricately carved staircase to connect the dining and drawing rooms was specially ordered by the Dame of Samarès to be in keeping with the two restored rooms.

In the past there were certain services that not only the Seigneur had to give the king but that tenants had to give their lord of the manor. In Samarès tenants in the fief had to defend the person of their Seigneur in times of danger with their own body, and even stand hostage for him. Each tenant had also once in his life to ship his lord and master to any one of four Norman ports whenever he wanted a free trip to France. Four 'voluntary' journeys per vassal! As late as 1763 tenants had the menial tasks of making the Seigneur's hay and cleaning out his *colombier*.

The rector of St Clement had his own special duty too, though this by its very nature occurred quite infrequently. If the Dame of Samarès happened to have a baby while living in the fief du Hommet, a subsidiary of the Samarès fief, then it was the rector's task to make sure that the dame had a white horse on which to ride to church for her christening service.

The present Seigneur of Samarès no longer has the privileges his ancestors enjoyed, such as chasing rabbits over the Town Hill, but he still has a duty in common with some other Seigneurs. Once a year he has to attend L'Assize d'Héritage. This is a sitting of the Heritage Division of the Royal Court, which certain Seigneurs attend and when the name of their fief is called affirm their allegiance to the Queen. This is the oldest court still attended in Europe.

Le Hocq

A beach which is popular with local families is further east around the coast at Le Hocq (*Bus 1*), just opposite St Clement's Parish Hall. It extends quite a distance both sides of the slipway and is sheltered from the north wind by the high sea wall. There is a grassy picnic area for those who do not want sand in their sandwiches and when the weather is good a van serves light refreshments and ice creams. Here, too, can be found St Clement's Millennium Cross. Bathing here is safe and best at high tide. At low tide this is a favoured spot for those fishing, with salt and plastic bags, for razor fish. Feeding on an incoming tide during the winter months waders are prolific, including plover, redshank, turnstone, dunlin, curlew, oyster catcher and large numbers of black-bellied brent geese.

There is also pleasant sailing for windsurfers at high water in St Clement, but sailors should be warned about the dangerous currents at low tide.

Other Places of Interest in St Clement

For those who want something other than windsurfing, swimming or walking there are the **Jersey Recreation Grounds** (*Bus 2c, 1*) which are on the corner made by the Inner Road at Grève d'Azette and Plat Douet Road. Here there is a variety of sports for all ages where the whole family can relax and enjoy a day in the open air. For serious golfers there is a 9-hole course, and golf clubs are available for hire if needed. Less serious golfers can opt for either mini-golf or putting where equipment is supplied. There are sixteen courts for tennis players and racquets and balls can be hired. There are also bowling greens. Patrons can relax and enjoy a snack or a full meal, hot or cold, from breakfast time onwards, inside or outside on the patio of the fully licensed self service café which is open all the year round. Special parties can be catered for too. There are also changing and shower facilities in the same building. ☎ 01534 721938

For those who prefer their sports from a spectator's point of view, the entrance to the **FB Playing Fields**

Le Hocq, a popular beach with a grassy picnic area.

(*Bus 2c*) is just a short distance away on La Grande Route de St Clement (A5) which is to be found by turning left at the traffic lights near the Recreation Grounds. Named after Florence Boot, the wife of the famous chemist, there are football and cricket pitches as well as Jersey's all-weather six-lane athletics track with facilities for all field events which was opened in September 1987 by the Olympic gold medallist David Hemery.

The track can be used by visiting athletes, but rubber sole shoes or 6mm needle spikes only should be worn. It is available daily till dusk for running, long and triple jump and general training. Hurdles, high jump, pole vault and throwing equipment, however, are available to authorised athletes only.

☎ 01534 759610

The final spot for visitors to this parish to make for is its centre – **St Clement's parish church** (*Bus 2c*). It is further to the east, along La Grande Route de St Clement, the Inner Road. The name Clement comes from the Latin *clemens*, meaning merciful, and it was a very popular name in ecclesiastical circles in the Middle Ages. The Clement, however, from whom both the church and the parish got their name was probably Pope Clement I, who lived in the first-century AD. He is best known for his Epistle to the Church of Corinth and has long been the patron saint of sailors – most appropriate for a parish with such a dangerous coastline. St Clement's special emblem, which is also the parish crest, is an anchor, to commemorate his being condemned to die for his faith by drowning in the Black Sea, with an anchor tied round his neck.

The date of the original St Clement's church is hard to pinpoint, as it has been so altered and added to over the centuries, but it could not have been later than 1067. From 1090 to the time of the Reformation it was owned by the abbey of St Sauveur le Vicomte in Normandy, which was responsible for its upkeep. At this time, in common with the other parish churches, it would have been a building with a low thatched roof and narrow windows, two of which can still be seen in the north wall. That part of the present church where the organ is now was a separate chapel and remained so for about 500 years. The fine sculptured granite font dates from about 1400 and was dumped outside the church during the Reformation, only being found again 300 years later.

In the fifteenth and sixteenth centuries the church gradually took the cruciform shape it has today and added its belfry and spire. The church's renowned wall paintings date back to the fifteenth-century and are worth looking at for their period detail. On the west wall of the south transept all that remains of an illustration of an ancient French poem are the legs of two horses, the hand of one of its riders, the head of a dog and the depiction of a boar, which presumably was being hunted. The poem, *The Three Living and Three Dead*, tells how three successful hunters met three skeletons who warned them of the vanity of worldly success and pleasure. All that is left on the wall of the French text reads 'Alas, St Mary, who are these three corpses who look so grim? It breaks my heart to see them so piteous.'

The walls in the north transept and on the north side of the nave tell the tales of two vanquished dragons. In the first St Margaret holds the wing of the one she conquered, while St Michael has just slain his in the second.

During the hundred years or so that followed the break from Catholicism in the sixteenth-century, St Clement's church, in common with the island's eleven other parish churches, was no longer referred to as a church but as a temple. It was whitewashed every 10 years or so and instead of coming in to worship together, the men of the parish used the west door and the women used a door, now walled up, at the end of the north transept. No equal rights in Jersey's Calvinist period!

Today, the church still retains its rural setting, with cows grazing in the fields that stretch down to the churchyard. The inn, which is to the west of the church, was built on the site of one of the four priories founded here soon after the original parish churches were built – hence its name, The Priory.

Grouville

Around the Parish

Fame has come to Grouville in several guises – from Neolithic times to the present day. For many centuries both pagan and Christian pilgrims came to the parish to worship at La Hougue Bie; today's visitors to the parish come in their thousands especially to watch Jersey pottery being made. And over the intervening years there have been other compelling reasons to come to Grouville.

The most ancient of the landmarks in this south-eastern parish, with its long eastern coastline, is a Neolithic burial chamber, covered by a mound that is over 40ft (12m) high. This cruciform passage grave of **La Hougue Bie** (*Bus 3a*) is considered to be one of the finest dolmens in Europe. By the time the site was excavated in 1924, though, it had already been robbed, but the religious vase supports that still remained suggested that it had been a religious monument of some importance.

The huge mound which covers this ancient burial place has given it its name, as 'Hougue' is a corruption of *haugr* – the Norse word for mound. The meaning of the adjective 'Bie' is harder to trace, but the legend which purports to give it its origin shows the continuing religious tradition surrounding La Hougue Bie down to Christian times.

La Hougue Bie, with its Neolithic grave, its two chapels and crypt are now owned by La Société Jersiaise and cared for by the Jersey Heritage Trust. Further attractions for visitors have been added to in the grounds which extend between Prince's Tower Road (B28) and La Rue des Pigneaux (B46). There is a clear plan at the entrance to show exactly where all the different museum sections are in relation to La Hougue Bie itself. To the left of the entrance is the **Archaeological and Geology Museum**, which has among its many fascinating exhibits a few coins from the hoard of 2,500 dating back to 56BC, which were discovered by a Grouville farmer on his land at the end of the 1950s. Archaeological finds in the island from most periods are represented here: the mammoth tusk and tooth from La Cotte de St Brelade from prehistoric times, and on the wall the carved corbels

*La Hougue Bie, the entrance passageway
of the prehistoric chambered tomb.*

La Hougue Bie Chapel.

La Hougue Bie, the apple crusher, picnic area and museum building.

that come from the ruined Grosnez Castle in St Ouen which dates back to about the fourteenth-century.

The Geology Gallery is situated in the basement of the Archaeological Museum and is clearly displayed and explained. It shows Jersey's geological setting in the Armorican area of which it is a part.

One attraction did not have to be added at La Hougue Bie, because it was already there – the **German Command Bunker** which was sited at the foot of La Hougue Bie at the time of the German Occupation of Jersey (1940–5). For some years this has been used as an Occupation Museum but redevelopment work has been carried out to create a unique and permanent memorial dedicated to World War II slave workers in the Channel Islands.

'The Land Map' charts the numerous buildings, monuments and other features of Jersey's landscape that have for centuries been regarded as special and sacred. The history and significance of many of these has been lost or forgotten.

The complex at La Hougue Bie includes a museum shop where posters, books and postcards and light snacks can be bought. There are also toilet facilities in the grounds and room for parking. Only part of the site is accessible for disabled visitors. To reach La Hougue Bie, follow the A6 or A7 from St Helier to the Five Oaks roundabout, then bear right on to the B28 and continue for approximately 1 mile (1.6km).

La Rocque

La Rocque harbour (*Bus 1*) on the south-east corner of Grouville will retain its fame as the place where in 1781 French

troops got ashore unchallenged – the last French invasion the island had to suffer. Just before midnight on Friday 5 January 1781, thirty small boats cautiously approached La Platte Rocque. They were being skilfully piloted through the hazards of that treacherous coastline by a renegade parishioner from Grouville. Yet everyone else on board was French and under the command of Baron de Rullecourt, who wanted to conquer Jersey for Louis XVI of France.

The 4-hour-long disembarkation took place on the sands at low tide and went unchallenged because the Chef de Garde had been so busy celebrating the eve of Twelfth Night that he had forgotten to post a sentry at La Rocque battery or to send out patrols along that part of the coast. Before all could be got ashore, however, the fast incoming tide prevented the landing of not only the drummers, but, more importantly, the gunners. So de Rullecourt, without meeting any resistance, left a small force at La Rocque to cover his retreat and led less than a thousand men through the deserted country lanes to St Helier.

By about 5.30am that morning the French invaders had got as far as Colomberie without even the night watchman apprehending them. In fact, the first casualties of the invasion were innocent victims in St Helier who happened to look out of their houses at the sound of marching feet. Once at Hill Street, de Rullecourt divided his troops to form an attack on the Royal Square from two sides and by 6.40am the French invaders had captured the centre of St Helier without meeting any military resistance whatsoever.

De Rullecourt then ordered the Lieutenant-Governor, Moses Corbet, who was still in bed, to meet him at what is now the Royal Court in the Royal Square. At the meeting, the French commander demanded the surrender of the rest of the island, threatening that the alternative was wholesale slaughter and pillage by the 4,000 troops he had at his command. Falling for this bluff, Moses Corbet surrendered.

However, while de Rullecourt was proclaiming himself the new Governor of Jersey and planning a celebration dinner at Government House, rebellious forces at Elizabeth Castle and Westmount were refusing to lay down their arms. By 11.30am, the 3,000 troops on Westmount were being organised by the young English Major Peirson, to swoop down on the Royal Square, where the invaders were now cooped up. By midday the Battle of Jersey had begun in the Royal Square, but, just at the point of victory, the gallant Major Peirson was mortally wounded and did not live to see the complete rout of de Rullecourt and his forces. De Rullecourt also died that same day, just 24 hours after he had landed so confidently at La Rocque.

Back in Grouville, the invasion remained undetected for several hours until the officer in charge of Fort Conway (now Fort Henry) received a message from St Helier. Urged on by the rector of St Martin, Captain Campbell sent a troop of 120 grenadiers to attack the French troops left behind at La Rocque. A platoon of forty men led by Lieutenant Robertson were the first to arrive on the coast and immediately started to attack the enemy, despite being outnumbered by them. Though the battle was small, heavy casualties were sustained, with loss of life on both sides. A memorial to the seven men in Robertson's platoon who died can be seen to the right of the west door in the churchyard of Grouville church. A plaque at La Rocque commemorates the invasion.

La Rocque is a typical fisherman's harbour with its sea walls — the oldest on the island — and its nineteenth-century granite pier. The beach which faces south is a sandy one with safe bathing at high tide and at low tide a 2-mile (3.25km) stretch of beach is left exposed for rock clambering and exploring. Visitors should, however, be extremely careful not to get stranded on the rocks by the swift inrush of the sea, especially at the time of the spring tides which occur every month shortly after the new and the full moon. Limited parking and toilet facilities are available at La Rocque. An added attraction is to watch the fishermen bringing back their catches.

Although unsuccessful, the French invasion made the islanders determined to fortify this vulnerable east coast against any further attacks. Thus it is that so many towers can still be seen in Grouville. Seymour Tower was completed the following year, in 1782, on L'Avarison islet about 1½ miles (2.4km) off La Rocque Point. It replaced an earlier tower, which probably accounts for the fact that it is square — unique among Jersey's coastal towers. It stands in lonely isolation on the horizon and is accessible at low tide, but visitors should take extreme care not to be trapped there by the rapidly returning tide. This happened in 1987 to two riders and their horses and their dangerous plight in having to

La Rocque harbour.

stay overnight in the tower until low tide the following day was reported not just locally but by the UK news media as well. Adventurous visitors can now make a planned overnight stay through Jersey Walk Adventures; ☎ 01534 853033. Other towers which were hastily built to defend the Grouville coastline were Platte Rocque Tower, Grouville No 1, Keppel Tower, Le Hurel, Fauvic and Grouville No 5. These were all put up by the States before 1794 but are now in private ownership, so visitors should take care not to invade the privacy of the present occupiers of these towers.

The Royal Bay of Grouville

Queen Victoria was so impressed by Grouville's east-facing coast, when she visited Jersey in 1859, that she sent a message to the Bailiff on her return to England that she would like it to be known in future as the Royal Bay of Grouville (*Bus 1, 2c*). And what a great deal of natural beauty there still is today – not just the sea and the sand, but also the common.

The bay offers nearly 5 miles (8km) of sandy beach – plenty of space for beach games and family picnics as well as safe bathing. The stretch of sand is also ideal for walking from Le Hurel slip, on the A4 in the south, to Gorey, or for the more energetic to jog along. The distance is about 4 miles (6.5km) and the return journey can be made by walking (or jogging) up Beach Road to the Gorey coast road, turning left and coming along the A4 road which runs through the common and through the woods back to Le Hurel.

Any winter walker will be delighted by the sight of numerous wading birds

Above and below: Jersey Pottery, Gorey.

on the shore overwintering here, such as brent geese, curlew, redshank and plover: summer walkers can spot the common and sandwich tern as well as the oyster-catcher which breed here during the warmer months.

In the centre of the bay is the **Gorey Watersports Centre**. Here watersports enthusiasts can try wake-boarding and waterskiing. Alternatively, they can venture out in a fun-canoe, a glass-bot-tomed boat (self-drive) or on a banana boat – or just enjoy being taken for a speedboat ride. The centre, which is only open in July and August, has a guardboat in case anyone experiences any difficulty. This is certainly a beautiful setting, with Gorey Castle as a backdrop.

Grouville Bay is just the right shel-tered spot when the wind is from the south-west or north and, for those who do not like sand in their sandwiches, there is the alternative of the common which runs along the length of most of the beach for picnicking. To the left from the beach and the common the rugged splendour of Mont Orgueil can be seen, together with Gorey's picturesque quay and waterfront – an ideal subject for photographs. There is ample parking space and there are cafés and kiosks along the beach. Toilets are sited at the coast end of Beach Road, just past Fort William.

The Germans, during the Occupa-tion, made extensive use of Grouville Bay. They realised that the texture of its sand was ideal for making the concrete needed to turn Jersey into an impreg-nable fortress. To facilitate the moving of the sand, the Germans built a railway from Gorey to St Helier. By the end of the Occupation over a million tons of Grouville beach had been used in the miles of concrete defences the Germans built over the island.

The 71 acres (29 hectares) of common land which flank the beach have been popular with islanders over the centuries for several different reasons. In the eigh-teenth-century **Grouville Common** (*Bus 1, 1b*) was the favourite spot for duels. In 1843 the horse races which were first run on St Aubin's sands and then at Grève d'Azette were moved to Grouville Common. So success-ful was the move that for 60 years all horse racing took place here, together with a splendid carnival complete with sideshows and stalls. The Jersey painter, Ouless, in 1849, captured the feeling of it in his famous painting *The Jersey Races*. This now hangs in the Jersey Museum, where postcard reproductions of the colourful scene are also available.

An important part of Grouville today, as far as conservationists are concerned, is the flat, fresh water marsh behind Gorey Common, known as **Grouville Marsh**. Though much reduced in size from what it once was, throughout the spring it still retains a good amount of fresh water, so providing the perfect habitat for winter-ing ducks, such as teal and shoveller as well as grey heron and common snipe. It is also visited in both spring and autumn by many migrating birds, including the reed, garden and willow warbler. It is also a breeding site for the great and lesser spotted woodpecker as well as the yellow wagtail. It is thought to be the best ornithological site on the island and a good viewing point is from La Cache des Prés off the A3. The flora is typical of a wetland area, featuring both reed and iris beds.

Another part of the common is the course which belongs to the **Royal Jersey Golf Club** (*Bus 1, 1b, 2c*). Many golfers might be familiar with the name Harry Vardon – the champion golfer who won the British Open Championship five times – but few may realise his connection with this course at Grouville. Harry Vardon had his early training at the Royal Jersey Golf Club, which had been established in the island as early as 1878, under the name of the Grouville Golf Club. Other players who began here include Ted Ray and the Ryder Cup Player Tommy Horton.

Visitors are welcome to the 18-hole Royal Jersey Golf Club, but are subject to starting times which are in force when they play. Handicap certificates are required and they must also be members of a recognised golf club and should contact the club early in their holiday if they want a game, as the sport is very popular.

Gorey Village

The tiny shopping centre of the parish is Gorey Village (*Bus 1, 1b*), across the road from the common. Here, as well as Jersey Pottery, there are several small shops including a newsagent, a grocer and a chemist. The village has an old world charm and is best explored on foot to take in the architectural details that are particularly 'Jersey', such as the dormer windows with their glazed sides and decorated bargeboards or gables. This is certainly the appropriate place to buy tomatoes, as the parish is famous for growing them.

The famous novelist Mary Ann Evans, better known as George Eliot, who came to Jersey in 1857 for a 3-month holiday, stayed in Gorey Village. After she and her companion had checked into the Union Hotel in the Royal Square as Mr and Mrs George Lewes, the couple later took lodgings in the house in the main road, now known as 'Villa Rosa'.

George Eliot wrote of the time they spent at Rosa Cottage, as it was then called, as 'a sweet, peaceful life'. In the evenings she and Lewes strolled by the sea, preferring the common to the beach itself as 'you can have the quietest, easiest walking'. They also watched the races and saw there, as the novelist puts it, 'a little of Jersey human nature'. Here, at Rosa Cottage, Eliot wrote *Janet's Repentance*, the third of her *Scenes of Clerical Life* short stories.

By mid-July George Eliot was finding the heat too much for her and so they decided to return to England. Though they had both found Jersey 'disappointingly English in habits and prices', Eliot summed up their impressions of 'such grassy valleys in this delicious island' as 'a sweet spot in our memories'.

The largest pottery in the Channel Islands, **Jersey Pottery** (*Bus 1, 1b*), is in the main road, Gorey Village and with its Egon Ronay recommended Garden Restaurant and Spinnakers Bar and Grill, it is definitely a place to visit.

There are two different methods of making the pottery and the open-plan layout, together with the clear explanations of the different stages on the walls, make it easy to follow exactly what happens from the raw clay stage to the finished product. The casting method begins in the mould-making studio, where plaster of Paris moulds are made of the item required. The next stage is

Queen's Valley.

for semi-porcelain to be poured into the mould and left to dry. Any decoration is then hand-painted onto the shape before it is glazed and put into the kiln for firing.

The Museum charts the history and development of the pottery since 1946. Glaze Craze is a 'paint it yourself' studio, which is popular with both adults and children. Here visitors can purchase a blank piece of pottery and decorate it with their own design. It will then be glazed and fired by the Pottery and be ready for collection in 3 to 4 days.

The climax of this family-owned complex is the showroom, where nearly 200 different lines of pottery, which are made on the premises in their various colour combinations, are put on display. There is everything here from tiny candlesticks to large lamp stands. Popular items with visitors are the traditional Jersey items such as the bean crock, the milking can and anything featuring the gentle Jersey cow. Those objects which cannot be carried home can be carefully packed and posted by the Pottery. Jersey Pottery can only be bought in the Channel Islands and, as well as being on sale at the Pottery itself, can only otherwise be bought in their shop in Bond Street, and Halkett Place, St Helier or in Guernsey.

The Pottery has three cafés in St. Helier, at Liberation Square, 59–61 King Street and the Café and Noddle Bar at 5 Colomberie Street; although some of the pottery items are displayed here, they are not for sale.

Jersey Pottery is also a place to eat and somewhere to relax, for it has a first- class restaurant where meals can be eaten inside or out, plus attractive gardens laid out round patios, pools and a fountain, with seating in the shade and in the sun. The Pottery is clearly signposted on the main St Helier–Gorey road going east, with plenty of space for cars at the back of the complex. Disabled visitors will find that ramps and special facilities have been provided for them. Visitors could easily spend half a day here, there is so much to see and enjoy.

Inland Grouville

The parish of Grouville is not just eastern and southern coastlines, impressive though those may be. It has always been noted for its agriculture and its inland pathways. Going back to an old agricultural practice, when Jersey's grain was ground by either wind or watermill, in this parish is the island's oldest windmill, whose history can be traced as far back as 1331. Now sailless, and adjoining a private residence, it is still preserved, to the west of the B37, as a landmark to help ships navigate the reef-strewn waters over which it looks.

Once the site of three working watermills, and now turned into the island's third reservoir, is **Queen's Valley** (*Bus 3a*), which lies behind Jersey Pottery. With the construction of this reservoir,

the island now has an extra storage capacity, holding about 260 million gallons of water (1,182 million litres). This now, from its own catchment area together with surplus water pumped from other areas, yields 450 million gallons (2,046 million litres) a year, an increase in the total reservoir storage of a 80 per cent.

A bonus to the walker is that the reservoir has not only been carefully planned to preserve as much of the natural environment as possible, but that a walk has been laid out around it too. This walk follows the natural contours of the land and has many seats sited at scenic spots along its route. Certainly the extensive planting of trees and shrubs, together with the use of local granite to clad the concrete structures within the boundary of the reservoir, has done much to retain the rural charm of the valley.

Visitors keen on fishing will be interested to know that this sport is actively encouraged by the waterworks company, as the reservoir is stocked with trout as a means of monitoring the quality of the water being stored.

Both walkers and fishermen coming to the valley by car will find parking areas at either end of the reservoir. Unfortunately, though, parts of the 2-mile (3.25km) walk are not suitable for wheelchair users.

On the way to the Reservoir from Chemin des Maltières is the manor farm once known as La Maletière, as it belonged from 1170 to the Malet family. It has one of the best examples on the island of a spiral stone staircase and, incredibly, in its 800-year-old history, it has only been sold twice. The manor, now known as **Les Prés Manor**, has been in the present owner's family since 1841 and the grounds are open to the public on such occasions as the annual church garden party in September.

Having established Grouville's claims to fame then and now, it is interesting to speculate how it got its name, because it is the only parish whose name does not have a religious association. The old form of Grouville was Grosville. This would suggest that, as ville or villa merely meant a farm with the land attached to it, someone on the south-east of the island had a particularly large (*gros*) farm which eventually gave its name to the whole district.

Although **Grouville parish church** is always spoken of as Grouville, its full title is the parish church of St Martin de Grouville. So St Martin of Tours is the patron saint of both Grouville's and St Martin's parish church, though the latter is the older dedication of the two. The saint's story is depicted in the east window of the north chapel, with the first panel showing the well-known incident of St Martin sharing his cloak with a beggar. Again, unusually for Jersey, although the oldest part of most island churches is the chancel, with Grouville it is the nave, which is thought to be over 1,000 years old. Its antiquity can be judged from the stones obviously brought up from the beach which make its walls.

Items worthy of note inside the church are the church plate, which includes the work of local silver smiths dating back to the seventeenth-century, the font and the *bénitier*. The eight-sided font has a curious design as well as a strange history. Made of Chausey granite sometime in the Middle Ages it has a double bowl, the smaller bowl perhaps intended to catch the water from the baby's head as it was baptised, so that it would not contaminate the holy water in the larger bowl.

At the time of the Reformation it was thrown out of the church and was discovered in 1650, with another font, being used in a farmyard as a pig trough. Both fonts were brought to the town church to be placed there, but the strict Calvinist congregation refused to let them in to what they called their 'temple'. The double-bowled font was then lost sight of for nearly 200 years, when it unexpectedly appeared, in a painting of about 1830, lying abandoned in the grounds of La Hougue Bie. When La Hougue Bie was bought by La Société Jersiase, it gave the font back to its rightful owner, Grouville church. Only the bowl, whose rim has had to be restored, is original; the plinth on which it stands is modern.

Next to the lectern is what is generally believed to be a holy water stoup, or *bénitier*. It has a stone bowl with a heart-shaped outlet and the letters 'IHS' carved on the side, the Greek initials for the name of Jesus.

Outside the church, as well as the monument to the grenadiers killed attacking the rearguard of the French invasion forces at La Rocque, are marks which indicate the uses to which an island parish church was put until this century. The west door has been made extra wide for wheeling out the parish cannon and there are also stones marking where the upper school door used to be. Booklets are available on request which, though written for children, reveal fascinating detail about the church to any visitor.

Places to Visit

Jersey Pottery & Restaurants

Gorey Village, Grouville

☎ 01534 851119

www.jerseypottery.com

Open: 7 days a week all year except for the Christmas holidays. Spinnakers Bar & Grill is open 7 days a week, including Fri and Sat evenings ☎ 01534 850831 for reservations. Winter opening times may vary.

La Hougue Bie Museum

La Hougue Bie, Grouville

☎ 01534 853023

www.jerseyheritage.org

Open: 1 April to 31 Oct 10am–5pm. Includes Archaeology and Geology Museum. Memorial to World War II slave workers of the Channel Islands.

Reduced admission charge for senior citizens and students; children under 6 free.

Les Prés Manor

Grouville

Grounds open occasionally for charity.

Samarès Manor and gardens

Inner Road, St Clement

☎ 01534 870551

www.samaresmanor.com

Open: daily early Apr to mid-Oct 10am–5pm

Spectacular gardens, manor house, museum, dovecote and nursery. Activities for the whole family.

Admission Charge.

3. St Martin and Trinity

Around St Martin

The parish of St Martin has always been dominated by its church, its castle and its manor. So it is not surprising that the major building developments in this mainly rural parish centre round the church, Gorey Castle and the small harbour to which the manor has given its name of Rozel. It is, though, probably confusing to the visitor to find that Gorey and Rozel are in two different parishes. Gorey Castle and harbour are in St Martin, but most of Gorey Village is in Grouville. With Rozel, the harbour and the manor are in St Martin, but the western part is in Trinity.

Though both **St Martin's parish church** (*Bus 3, 3a*) on La Grande Route de Rozel, and Grouville's are dedicated to the same saint, the former is always mentioned in records as St Martin the Old, and the earliest mention of it dates back to 1042. It was also considered to be Jersey's leading church, not just because of the size of its endowments but because it provided so many of the island's Deans.

A glance at the outside of the church will show an amazing number of buttresses, some even made of tombstones. This was because the walls were built only sufficiently strong to support the original thatched roof. When a stone roof was added, the stability of the walls was endangered and in both the sixteenth and eighteenth centuries it had to be given extra support.

Another part of the church's structure which caused problems was its spire. One Sunday morning in 1616, just as the congregation were going to church, the spire was struck by lightning and broke in two. This caused a great deal of panic in the parish, as parishioners thought that this act of God was the forerunner of worse evil about to befall the island, because they fervently believed that 'Judgement must begin at the House of God'. The spire rebuilt in 1618 was struck by lightning too – in 1837.

What can also be noticed from outside, by looking at the south wall, is where the earliest part of the church originally was and where a later addition was made. The chancel at the east end was the original chapel from which the parish church sprang and has its walls built of boulders taken from the beach. The later, western extension of the south wall is made of quarried stone and has a higher roof.

St Martin's *perquage* or sanctuary path went from the church and followed a stream which finally came out at St Catherine's Bay. The last recorded criminal to use it was Thomas Le Seeleur, who, in 1546, preferred exile in Normandy to a death by hanging in the island of his birth. The path, from the church through Rozel Woods to St Catherine's Tower, makes a pleasant if rather muddy walk which can be enjoyed by holidaymakers in a rather different spirit from those for whom the escape route was originally intended.

To walk the sanctuary path in reverse, park the car at White Tower on the B29 to St Catherine. Walk out of the car park turning left onto the B29. Take the first turning to the right and then in about 200yds (183m) take a track to the left. This leads to, and by the side of, the Mazeline Reservoir which was constructed by the Germans during the Occupation. The path now follows the stream through delightful woodland, where the yellow iris, foxglove, red campion and buttercup grow in profusion. In spring and early summer the woods are alive with birdsong.

The stream is crossed and recrossed by stepping stones. At the walled path keep to the left and continue upwards, until the sign 'La Becterie' on the wall on the left. Now turn right into Rue de Belin, which passes the large Methodist chapel and leads to La Grande Route de Rozel; turn left and walk along to the parish church, which completes the route of the sanctuary path.

This is a good resting place, or refreshments can be taken at the local tavern. Now retrace the route until the second turning on the right, La Rue des Vaux de l'Eglise. There are some interesting properties along this lane and also a fine *lavoir*. The hinge pivots either side would suggest that this public place for washing linen once had doors, with the stonework at the side for beating the washing dry. Follow the winding lane uphill, turning left into Rue des Charriers, which continues downhill. As you are about to turn left to join the B29 to St Catherine and the car park, notice the fountain on the right, set into a wall with its tiny granite trough and 3½ft (1m) high pillar, which would have been used as a spout for a purpose now forgotten. Walking time 1 hour. Moderate hills.

As a Millennium project, St Martin's Parish has taken steps to ensure that all the old and existing footpaths within the Parish are clearly signposted.

Built over 150 years later than the church was **Mont Orgueil (Gorey Castle)** *(Bus 1, 1b)*, on a rugged promontory which had once been the site of a large Iron Age hillfort. Started sometime between 1180 and 1212 on the orders of England's King John, it commanded the Normandy coastline from Cap de la Hague to Coutances from where any threatened invasion would come.

To begin with, the castle was simply known as Gorey Castle, which it is still called today, but, at the beginning of the fifteenth-century, Henry V's brother, the Duke of Clarence, was so impressed by the castle's unique position and great strength that he called it Mont Orgueil (Mount Pride), a name which it also bears, for this medieval island defence was one of the finest ever built. It was constructed on the concentric principle, with each stage of the fortification independent of the rest. For even greater impregnability, the walls wherever possible come straight out of the rock, so that the combination of stone wall and rock presented any would-be attacker with almost insuperable obstacles at every level. Morever, there is not just one but five gates to breach, each one higher up than the last, with drawbridges to cross to the first two, until the keep itself is reached.

Mont Orgueil's ten towers and two machicolated bastions – where boulders and pitch could be poured through holes in the floor onto the invaders coming up from below – were not in place or complete in the twelfth-century. They were gradually added and modified through the next three centuries in increasing efforts to defend the island against the French. The castle was beseiged by them in 1338 and 1339; nearly taken in 1373, but an English fleet arrived just in time; French troops, however, did finally get in through the treachery of a postern being left open in 1461. The importance of the castle in the island's defence is proved by this French victory – once French troops were in the castle, they managed to stay in it for 7 years and virtually ruled the rest of the island from it. It took Richard Harliston in 1468 – with the help of the rebelling islanders – 19 weeks to get the French garrison to surrender and finally liberate Jersey from the invaders.

With the exception of this 7-year French occupation, Mont Orgueil had proved impregnable from attack by armies which relied on bows and arrows and knights in armour. Quite the reverse was true when cannon were introduced. The castle had not been built either to withstand cannon shot nor to have cannon positioned inside it. Worse than that, it was overlooked by Mont St Nicolas, just 400ft (122m) away, from which enemy artillery could have bombarded it with impunity. So, in 1593, the English military engineer Paul Ivy suggested that no more money should be spent on Gorey Castle, but that a new castle, to defend the fast growing town of St Helier, should be built in St Aubin's Bay.

In the normal course of events, Mont Orgueil would have been razed to the ground to make it unusable, but that it still exists to dominate Jersey's eastern coastline today is due to Sir Walter Ralegh. When he was Governor of Jersey, he wrote to Queen Elizabeth, whose final decision it was: 'It is a stately fort of great capacity. It were a pity to cast it down.'

In the centuries following its reprieve, it has played an important role in the island's history no fewer than three times. In the English Civil War it took the part of King Charles and was under the command of the Governor's wife, Lady Philippe de Carteret, while Sir Philippe himself held out in Elizabeth Castle. Only after the king's defeat at the battle of Worcester was Mont Orgueil handed over to the Parliamentary troops.

During the French Revolution, the castle was the centre of another band of Royalist supporters, this time of the French king. Admiral Philippe d'Auvergne made the castle both a safe haven for escaping aristocrats and also the headquarters of an unsuccessful underground movement to restore the French monarchy.

Gorey Castle's final role was as part of Hitler's impregnable fortress, during the

Nazi Occupation of Jersey. The Germans constructed a large military headquarters and a machine gun post within the medieval fortification to defend the island against a British invasion.

Any visitor who goes inside the castle will soon realise from the information plaques that over the centuries it has been much more than a fort. In the early years the island was governed from here; its various lords, keepers and governors lived here. So there are two chapels inside the walls as well as residential apartments, the great hall and kitchen. Until 1693 the now ruined Busgros Tower was the island's prison, whose narrow stairs led down to a damp and noisome dungeon in which many prisoners died before they could be brought to trial. This was where, in the sixteenth and seventeenth centuries, the alleged witches were held – many on a starvation diet of bread and water.

Inside the castle there are also tableaux with taped explanations which span more than five centuries of the castle's history. The figures are sumptuously dressed and there is background music of the period to match. The small museum near the top of the castle displays archaeological finds dating from prehistory to the nineteenth-century.

As this historic building is built on a steep slope at several different levels reached by innumerable steps, it is not suitable for people with disabilities. However, wheelchair users are allowed in free to sit in the lower ward and to admire the colourful flower displays there, the views beyond the castle walls and to get some feel of the towering strength of the castle. The castle has recently undergone major refurbishment.

The grounds of **Rozel Manor** (*Bus 3*), off the B38, north of St Martin's church, are only open to the public occasionally for special events and charity functions. Visitors find the tall *Taxodium distichum* by the pond and the magnolia outside the chapel, both trees over a hundred years old, of particular interest. The manor itself is noteworthy both for the origin of its name and for the duties of the Seigneur to the visiting monarch.

'Rosel' is the old French for 'reed' and the Seigneurs of Rosel Castle in Normandy had three reeds as their arms. It was one of these Seigneurs in Norman times who was given a fief, a grant of land in Jersey from the King of England, and both the fief and the manor he built on it, including the bay it overlooks, were all given the name of Rosel or Rozel.

The duties of the Seigneur when his monarch came to Jersey were as follows: 'If the King come to this isle, you shall ride into the sea to meet him till the waves reach the girth of your saddle. And as long as he tarry in the isle, you shall act as his butler, and receive for your fee what the King's butler hath.' Today this duty is still carried out, but in more modern terms. When the Queen visits Jersey, after she has been received on landing by the Lieutenant-Governor and the Bailiff, the Seigneur of Rozel with the Seigneur of Augrès, who enjoys similar rights, are the first to greet her and welcome her to the island.

The present manor was built in 1770, but had the addition of the towers and turrets 50 years after. The *colombier* or dovecote and the chapel, both in the grounds, are much older, part of the latter going back to the twelfth-century. Rozel

Above: Mont Orgueil (Gorey Castle), showing the harbour at low tide.
Right: Mont Orgueil (Gorey Castle) and below Gorey harbour.

Prehistoric Sites

Those visitors who are interested in prehistory have two dolmens to visit in this parish. The oldest is **La Pouquelaye de Faldouët** (*Bus 3a and 1b – ask for top of Gorey Hill*), which goes back to about 2500BC. It is a developed passage grave with an intermediate design between the passage grave and the later simpler designs. So the chamber, with its 25-ton capstone, recalls the passage grave, but the area which opens up from it before  the passage is a new feature. The small cists in this open area were found to have cremated bones and late Middle Neolithic objects in them and originally had their own capstone.

The burial place is along La Rue des Marettes, up some steps and at the end of a narrow bush-lined lane. The grave itself is dominated by its huge capstone and beyond, through the trees, there is a view of the sea, as there so often is from these prehistoric sites.

The other dolmen in St Martin is to the north of the parish at Le Couperon, the **Dolmen du Couperon** (*Bus 3 to Rozel*). This gallery grave dates back to about 3250BC–2750BC and is only one of two of its kind in Jersey, the other being in St Helier. Originally the parallel-sided chamber was covered by a long, low mound, with the other stones forming a supporting wall at its base. The tomb was once divided by the porthole stone at the entrance, which, because of its size, would indicate that bones, rather than bodies, were laid in the upper part of the chamber.

Even someone not particularly interested in prehistory should try to visit this last resting place of some of Jersey's earliest inhabitants, with its wide view of the sea round to Telegraph Tower. It is reached by taking the road down to Le Saie Harbour and walking up along the bracken-lined footpath which branches to the left at the small space for car parking. Above the dolmen, Rozel Bay can be seen to the north-west, Le Saie Harbour just below, and everywhere the scent of wild flowers, as broom and wild honeysuckle grow in profusion in this tranquil spot.

Manor is off La Grande Route de Rozel, on the number 3 bus route.

A short distance from Rozel Manor, a little north of the junction of La Grande Route de Rozel and La Rue des Pelles, is Rozel Camp site. The site has 120 pitches, and the facilities include a shop, games room, television room and solar heated swimming pool.

Harbours and Beaches

Gorey Harbour and the Surrounding Area

St Martin is just the right parish for beachcombers and harbour hunters, for, between Gorey and Rozel and including them, there are at least ten delightful sea shores to track down.

On the south-east of the parish is **Gorey Harbour** (*Bus 1, 1b*) with its dominating backcloth of Mont Orgueil. The growth of this port from a mere fishing jetty to the harbour it has now become – boats ply between Jersey and the Normandy ports of Carteret and Port Bail from here – is the reason for the development of the whole area. It all started in the nineteenth-century with oysters.

There had always been an oyster bed just out to sea from Gorey which Jersey-men fished without competition until, at the beginning of the nineteenth century, they were joined by English boats from the south of England. By the mid-1830s at least 2,000 men and hundreds more women and girls were engaged in what had become such a profitable industry

that oysters were served free at all hotel meals.

The oyster industry lasted only 40 years or so – it destroyed itself by over-dredging – but the effects of it on this country parish were permanent. To accommodate the many English people engaged in the industry who could not understand a word of the French services held in the parish church, a church was built near the harbour specially for them, where the services would be in English. Many of the houses and cottages in Gorey also date from this time.

Shipbuilding was the next industry to bring prosperity to the parish with no fewer than seven shipyards stretching along the coast. By 1890, though, with the increasing use of steam-powered, iron-hulled boats, Jersey's shipbuilding boom was over. There is still, today, in the colourful gardens that line the promenade, a tangible record of Gorey's boatyards – a stone monument represents the keel of a ship on the stocks.

Situated at number 15 Gorey Harbour is the **Interpretation Centre**. Exhbition boards display information on the history of Gorey from prehistoric to modern times. No admission charge.

So, as well as a picturesque and lively harbour, where **The Jersey Jewellery Warehouse** can be found, Gorey has a nineteenth-century church, a small shopping area and a delightful walk along the flower-lined prom. What it does not have is ample parking space, so it might be as well to park somewhere along the common in the free parking zones and walk the short distance in.

After Gorey, going north along the coast, come several beaches before St Catherine is reached. **Petit Portelet**

(*Bus 1b*), just behind the castle, is tiny, pebbly and an ideally secluded picnic spot. It is reached by a footpath to the north of the fourteenth-century *mâchicoulis* (machicolation), misnamed by the Victorians 'Caesar's Fort.' Half a mile (0.8km) further along La Route de la Côte is the charmingly situated **Anne Port** (*Bus 1b*) with a beach extending both sides of the slipway. Here there is shingle and a wide stretch of sand with rising ground on three sides providing perfect shelter from all but an off-sea east wind. The bathing is also safe. There are toilet facilities but the parking – on one side of the slipway only and on one side of La Route d'Anne Port – though free, is limited.

Parking is not quite so much of a problem at **Archirondel** (*Bus 1b*), the next beach round, for there is a new car park to the left of the narrow lane leading to the cove, as well as parking space at the bottom of it. This delightful and sheltered spot with its rocky outcrops for scrambling, its shelving shingle and stretch of sand at low tide is certainly worth a visit.

The eighteenth-century defence tower on the left of the cove, now painted red as a landmark, juts out from what was once going to be the southern arm of a great harbour planned by the British Government for St Catherine's Bay as part of the war effort against France. The plan was, however, found to be impractical and never finished. Now only cormorants and other seabirds keep guard on the offshore rocks.

There is a small café here with toilet facilities, making this a good family beach. For walkers there is a coastal path to Fliquet which starts in the new car park in the lane, down the slipway. Pausing here, one can see right round the coast to Gibraltar slipway, where several local boats are moored, and beyond to Belval Cove. The unspoiled countryside that slopes gently away from this coastline, with its handful of classically proportioned houses, has probably hardly changed at all over more than a hundred years. For the technically minded, the large notice 'Power Cable', immediately to the left of this slipway at Archirondel, refers to the island's connection with the French electric grid, which enters Jersey at this point of the coast and goes to the rest of the island via the electricity station in the lane.

Archirondel is down a well signposted lane on the right of La Route de la Côte (B29) going towards St Catherine. This road, known as the pine walk, which leads to St Catherine is charmingly wooded with views of the bay through the trees. There are

Archirondel.

Fliquet

barbecue sites above Gibraltar slipway and just beyond Belval Cove where there is also a small car park on the other side of the road. Gibraltar itself is worth stopping at for the marked and photogenic contrast between the dark woods, which come down to the right of the slipway with its bobbing boats, and the lighter colour of the sea. In the woods in St Catherine's Valley grow plants unusual for Jersey, such as dog's mercury and yellow archangel.

St Catherine and the Surrounding Area

St Catherine (*Bus 1b*) is reached by a one-way system, on which are one or two laybys for parking and barbecue sites. Once at the headland, one's view is dominated by the almost ³/₄mile (1.25km) long breakwater. This was begun in 1847 and completed in 1855, at the instigation of the British Government, to be the northern arm of a large safe harbour for the British fleet in any altercation with France. The whole enterprise proved impractical and all that remains of the grandiose scheme is St Catherine's breakwater, which now belongs to the States of Jersey, and the short sea wall at Archirondel.

Today the breakwater is popular both for strolling along and fishing from. As it is built with two levels it is possible to walk out to sea on one level and come back on the other. On the way out Fliquet Bay and La Coupe Point can be seen on the left, the Ecréhous islets on the left horizon and the sweep of St Catherine's Bay to the right. There are plenty of seats *en route* from which to enjoy the seascape, as well as coin-in-slot rotating binoculars. For keen as well as casual anglers there are rods to hire and bait to buy from a small shop on the breakwater which is open from Easter until October from 10am to 8pm. There are toilet facilities at the top and bottom of the breakwater. Those at the bottom, however, are not accessible to wheelchair users.

There are also, on the headland, a café, a canoe club and a sailing club (members only).

Walkers can join the Archirondel to Fliquet walk to the left of the one-way system into St Catherine, just before the café, by the side of the layby. It is best to go along to Fliquet by the lower path and come back down the upper path – not so much of a climb. On this path there is a seat from which to see nearby France – not too clearly, though, or that would be a sign of coming rain!

At **Fliquet** itself there is a ridge under the eighteenth-century defence tower which makes an ideal picnic spot and limited parking on the roadway above. The beach is pebbly with rocks and suitable for picnics and explor-ing rather than bathing. There are no refreshment or toilet facilities, but not being much frequented is part of Fliquet's charm. Just beyond the tower, on the road which winds out of Fliquet, there is a house like a fairytale castle on the corner, which incorporates many of Jersey's typical granite architectural

features. Walkers will pass it on their way back to St Catherine by the footpath which starts again up the hill, on the left, marked by a wooden stile and from which panoramic views of France can be glimpsed. For drivers, Fliquet is down a well-signposted turning on the right, off the B91.

Up the twisting road from Fliquet, the road to the right at the first cross-roads leads to two more secluded spots – **La Belle Coupe** and Saie Harbour. The first turning to the right, Rue de la Coupe, winds down with Telegraph Hill rising up at the end of it. Here there is restricted parking with one footpath leading to the cliffs and the other down under hawthorn arches to La Belle Coupe. The tiny shingle and sand beach has a few steps leading down to it and is at its warmest in the morning, as it faces east. This is really the place to get away from it all.

Returning back up La Rue de la Coupe, the first turning to the right, La Rue de Scez, leads to **Saie Harbour** (also spelt 'Scez'). This beach is more open than La Belle Coupe and is not so good for bathing. It too, though, is not much frequented and affords plenty of opportunity for rock scrambling, col-lecting shells, winkling and limpeting and finding a sheltered niche in which to enjoy the expanse of sea stretching to the horizon. Brambles, sloe bushes and bracken go right down to the edge of the beach. An eye should always be kept on the tide, so that there is no danger of the sandy path along Saie Harbour leading to the slipway being covered by the swift inrush of the sea. A narrow track cut out of granite and the granite cobbled slipway were once used for collecting vraic (seaweed) with a horse and cart for growers to fertilise their *côtils*.

More backtracking is needed up La Rue de Scez for those in cars who wish to go on to Rozel, but for those on foot there is a public path called La Rue des Fontonelles – up the headland of Le Couperon, with its view across to the French coast, and past the dolmen which leads across the cliffs to the top of Rozel Hill.

Take the footpath, leaving the dolmen on the right, over the fast-flowing stream where watercress grows abundantly. From the top of the hill, a moderate climb, there is a good view across the bay to Rozel Fort above Rozel Harbour. Turn right into La Route de Rozel, passing Le Frère restaurant, and then there is the sweep down into **Rozel Bay**, one of the most attractive bays in Jersey. This walk should take about an hour.

Rozel

Rozel (*Bus 3*) itself lies in what appears to be a wooded amphitheatre and it has all the charm of a fishing village, including a refreshment kiosk along the waterfront as well as fishermen's cottages. It looks its best when the tide is up, with pleasure and fishing boats anchored in the harbour. When the tide goes out, it leaves a sandy beach along which waddle geese and ducks. There is also a rocky part of the beach away from the harbour which offers seclusion. Bathing is safe at all stages of the tide. Parking is often the worst part of visiting this north-eastern bay but there is parking just above the village up Le Chemin de

Guet. Just follow the signposts. While up this hilltop, to the west of the bay, note the great earth rampart about 20ft (6m) high and 30ft (9m) thick, the remains of a prehistoric promontory fort, called Castel de Rozel.

Back down in Rozel, it is well worth finding the road called Vallée de Rozel where the buses stop, just opposite the road leading to the beach in front of the hotel. This is a nature walk in miniature, especially in the spring, for over the road branch two spectacular trees – a pink tulip tree and the aptly nicknamed handkerchief tree, whose flowers resemble hankies. At the end of the road are fine examples of primulas growing by a tiny roadside stream at the approach to a private garden. The peaceful atmosphere all along this road was once shared by the whole of Rozel before it became so popular.

The rural charm of this walk can continue by turning left and going up Vallée de Rozel, past the willows grown specially for the making of baskets and the sweet chestnut trees that overhang the road. At the top of the steep hill is one of Jersey's remaining windmills, now sailless and standing in private grounds. It dates back at least to the sixteenth-century and was adapted by the Germans during the Occupation as an observation post.

Bannelais

St Martin's is the only parish which has kept up the ancient custom of *bannelais*. This means that throughout the year the road sweepings of leaves and twigs from this heavily wooded area of the island are stored for auctioning by the Constable in October. These

Rozel Bay.

Above: Rozel Bay Quay.

Above: Les Platons.

bannelais, or road sweepings, which are stacked at the top of St Catherine's Hill and at Carrefour-Baudains, can bring in as much as an extra £470 to the parish – no wonder that Grouville has also recently decided to renew this ancient Jersey custom.

Trinity

(Bus 3a, 3b, 4, 21)

This north-eastern parish, which lies between Rozel Bay and Havre Giffard and whose southern tip is only 2 miles (3.25m) from the Royal Square, is large and has a great fund of stories to match. The earliest have an element of magic and were all associated with the prehistoric remains that can be found along the northern coast of the parish.

Around the Parish

Starting on the north coast, on a rocky ledge overlooking Vicard Point, south of Petit Port, is a huge stone 15ft (4.5m) by 13ft (4m). This fallen menhir is known as **La Pierre de la Fêtelle**, the fairystone, as it seemed obvious to the descendants of prehistoric man that such a heavy object could only have got to its present position by magic! Vicard Point is on the coastal walk between Bouley Bay (*Bus 4*) and Bonne Nuit (*Bus 4*) and is clearly signposted.

Further west is the headland of **La Belle Hougue.** Two caves have been discovered here and are important archaeologically because of the fossil animal bones found in them, belonging most probably to the period just before the last Ice Age. Some of the remains belong to a special type of red deer and they can all be viewed at La Hougue Bie Museum in Grouville.

Inland from La Belle Hougue, to the highest point of the island, over 400ft (122m) above sea level, is **La Hougue des Platons**. Just north of the BBC transmitter and mast is a low prehistoric burial mound 3ft (0.9m) high, 36yd (23m) in circumference, under which was discovered a cist in which were two urns. In one of these were the charred remains of a woman and a child. La Hougue des Platons can be reached by going west along La Rue des Platons, and turning right, after La Rue d'Egypte, along a footpath across the common.

To walk to La Fontaine ès Mittes and La Hougue des Platons (see map page 2 and 3) take the footpath signposted to Bouley Bay. The path leads to the rocky promontory, La Belle Hougue, from where there are fine views of Guernsey, Sark, the French coast and Bonne Nuit Bay. Follow the path around the back and down the steps, where there is a signpost pointing to the right and the main road. Take the path to the left and walk straight on for 60yd (55m) and there on the left, behind the bracken and bushes is La Fontaine ès Mittes with its healing waters. Incidentally, the temperature of the water remains constant throughout the year.

Retrace the path to the sign to the main road and follow this grassy path which continues between hedges and banks. This path leads on to the lane Rue d'Egypte. Continue up Rue d'Egypte, turning right on to the grassy path, immediately after the entrance to 'Springfield'. Walk up this path for 100yd

(91m), then turn right, continuing over tussocky grass. Fifty yards (46m) in front is the tumulus, La Hougue des Platons. On the north side of this walled grassy mound is the pink granite reference stone.

To return to the car park, retrace the path to Route d'Egypte, to avoid trespassing on private property. After a short distance turn left, towards the sea, taking the path to the rocky promontory. From this point the cliff path can be seen below, so take either of the paths leading down to it. The walk back to the car park along the cliff path should take approximately 10 minutes. The whole walk should take about 1½ hours, is quite hilly and it is worth taking binoculars.

Next comes **Trinity church** (*Bus 4*) and one of the most picturesque ways to approach it is to come up from the south of the island along La Route de la Trinité. This is lined in part with silver birches and, just before the church, by a fine beech hedge Jersey cows can often be seen grazing in the water meadows to the right. Then the church itself comes into view, rather spoiled for some by the modern cement shell preserving its oddly proportioned spire.

In fact, the only parts of the church which date back to the twelfth-century are the spire and tower. The chancel was rebuilt a hundred years later and the nave, on the old medieval foundations, as recently as the middle of the nineteenth-century. Two relics of when Catholic services were held in the church are the silver chalice – the oldest in the island – and the wooden pews or misericords in the chancel, with their carved undersides which could be raised for the priests to lean against during long periods of standing in the lengthy services. The pews in the nave are of a Victorian type.

The whole church gives a feeling of light and air, but the seventeenth-century memorial to one of the important members of the de Carteret family, though probably the finest mural monument in the island, does seem rather too large for the dimensions of the fifteenth-century Lady Chapel.

Three unusual features of the church are that it only has one aisle; that its organ loft and choir are over the west door; and that it is the only island church not to be named after a saint. The belief in the Three in One nature of God – Father, Son and Holy Spirit – La Sainte Trinité to whom the church is dedicated, is the origin of the parish crest. The initials PFSD stand for *Pater, Filius, Spiritus Sanctus* and *Deus.*

The façade of Trinity Manor, however, is quite changed from how it must have looked in the seventeenth-century, as Athelstan Riley noted during its final restoration, in 1913, on the model of a small French *château.* The main door on the south front is the entrance to the original sixteenth-century house; the second front door, on the north side, is the entrance to the nineteenth-century rebuilding, in which the manor was exactly doubled in size.

Trinity Manor has now changed hands, and has a new Seigneur. The kennels of the island's Drag Hunt and Chase Club, which were once on the estate, have been moved to a new location in St Mary.

In this century the Seigneur's only remaining duty to his visiting sovereign is to offer the monarch a pair of mallard ducks – for which purpose ducks are always supposed to be reared in readiness on the manorial ponds. Unfortunately, for the Queen's visit in 1978, the Seigneur's own ducks' plumage did not look sufficiently colourful, so he had to borrow two from Gerald Durrell's zoo!

There are not many facilities for shopping in this northern parish and there are no banks. The only post office, which is also a general store, is near Trinity church. Two other general stores can be found in Victoria Village and at Les Hautes Croix, where La Grande Route de St Jean meets La Rue Militaire and Le Chemin des Hautes Croix. While in the Le Chemin des Hautes Croix area, visitors can watch a forge in action, on Route d'Ebenezer. The forge, which specialises in wrought iron work, is on a dangerous corner so visitors should park down the nearby side road, but not in front of the forge or the garage next door.

Pallot Steam Museum

Find Rue de Bechet (off A8 and A9) and explore the **Pallot Steam Museum**, which has rides in Victorian railway carriages two days a week. Don Pallot, who founded the museum, was a great enthusiast for steam. He died early in 1996, but his family are carrying on and extending the museum.

Pallot Steam Museum, showing a few of the exhibits.

Bouley Bay

Bouley Bay is a good starting point to explore Trinity's northern coastline and is reached by a steeply winding road down from La Rue de la Petite Falaise. The bay is named after the birch tree *(bouleau)* and is 2 miles (3.25km) across. To the east of it are hills over 400ft (122m) high and to the west the headland of La Belle Hougue. Such an ideal landing point for would-be invaders of the north of the island had to be defended and the fort at L'Etacquerel to the east and the Leicester Battery (named after Elizabeth I's Earl of Leicester) to the west still remain as part of that defence.

Some invaders over the centuries, nevertheless, did get through this line of defence and one was a French raiding party in 1549. Fortunately, once the invaders had got as far as Le Jardin d'Olivet, just above the bay, they were defeated, with a great number of French casualties. In 1643 the invading soldiers were English, sent by Cromwell to round up any Royalists who had not taken refuge in either Mont Orgueil or Elizabeth Castle.

Today Bouley Bay can be enjoyed either on its cliff tops or on its shingle beach, where the gorse and bracken covered hills come right down to the sea. The cliff path starts in Rozel and follows the cliffs past the disused L'Etacquerel Fort into Bouley Bay itself. This path can be joined on La Route de Rozel, or from the car park at Le Jardin d'Olivet.

The beach at Bouley Bay faces north-east and so is at its best before noon. It offers safe bathing in the harbour area, but families with small children should

Bouley Bay.

take care as the shore shelves quickly into deep water. Access to the beach is either down some steps or along the path by the beach café which links in with the coastal path from Rozel. There is also a small rocky beach to the left of the pier which would be ideal for a picnic when the tide is out. The pier itself was built in 1828, primarily for the oyster industry but also for defence. The initials of F. de la Mare, who was responsible for constructing it, can still be seen on the side of the harbour wall.

The pier is now a favourite spot for locals to fish, with conger in good supply in the summer nights and turbot and brill in the shorter days of autumn. Bouley Bay is also the place for discovering the sun-basking wall lizard.

Scuba Diving

The **Bouley Bay Dive Centre** (☎ 01534 866990) has 5 star PADI facilities. Here there are skin diving, boat dives and the possibility of hiring gear. Bottle filling facilities are also available. For swimmers, picnickers and divers there are toilet facilities, a café and limited parking.

Any cries and sceams heard round Bouley Bay in the summer are likely to be the excited cheers of spectators (and the roar of engines) as they line the road up from Bouley Bay for the four popular races known as the Bouley Bay Hill Climbs. The first is at Easter, the second on 9 May (Liberation Day), the third on the Spring Bank Holiday and the fourth in July. All are organised by the Jersey Motor Cycle and Light Car Club. The summer meeting is the most important of all, as it is the British Hill Climb Championship. The classes included in the various hill climbs are motor bikes, saloon cars, racing cars and sports cars. Even events for cycles and karts are held. These races are the only time when the essential tranquility of this northern bay is broken and they certainly make for thrilling viewing.

Bouley Bay affords a further walk to the west, to Belle Hougue Point and then round to Giffard Bay, the parish's western boundary. The keen walker can continue the 4 miles (6.5km) to Bonne Nuit in St John's parish or complete the north coastal walk to Grosnez in St Ouen. However far one walks, the views from the cliff tops are breathtaking: at Vicard Point there is the view back across to Bouley Bay; on the cliffs above Giffard Bay there is the long rock down below to the right which looks like the body of a man, giving the bay its nickname of Dead Man's Bay.

The headland of **La Belle Hougue** certainly lives up to its name of 'beautiful' with the sea on both sides, strange shapes of rocks at its peak and an atmosphere on a sunny day of tranquillity and changelessness. La Belle Hougue offers plenty of natural picnic sites on rock or grass and there are seats all along the coastal walk for those who like frequent rests. In the spring there is the added bonus of the slopes down to the sea being carpeted with daffodils, known locally as lent lilies. Later come the green fronds of the bracken with their distinctive scent. The paths around the headland pass by the spring, La Fontaine ès Mittes, at the end of the path known as Le Chemin de la Belle Hougue, and above the caves which have already been mentioned. Only experienced climbers, by the way, with the correct equipment including ropes and torches, should attempt to visit the two caves.

Augrès

Augrès (*Bus 4*) is one of the ancient fiefs into which Trinity is divided and is to the west of La Route de la Trinité (Trinity Road). On the way up to it is the Sir Francis Cook Art Gallery and in the grounds of Augrès Manor is Jersey's world-renowned zoo. Just past the zoo, to the west along La Rue des Câteaux, is an ancient earthwork.

Coming back to our own time, art lovers will be interested to learn about the **Sir Francis Cook Art Gallery** (*Bus 4*) which is at the top of Trinity Hill on La Route de la Trinité right next door to the Oaklands Lodge Hotel. There is a large car park behind the gallery, which was a former Methodist chapel and schoolroom, converted by Jersey resident and artist Sir Francis Cook and generously donated to The Jersey Heritage Trust by his widow in 1984.

Although there is no permanent exhibition housed at the gallery, there are a number of temporary exhibitions planned throughout the year, details of which will be found on the list of 'What's On' put out by the media. When these exhibitions are on, it is possible to view a selection of Sir Francis Cook's own paintings in two adjoining rooms.

The obvious focal point in this area is Augrès Manor, the home of author and naturalist the late Gerald Durrell. It is also the international headquarters of the Durrell Wildlife Conservation Trust,

formerly the Jersey Wildlife Preservation Trust, and also widely known as the **Jersey Zoo** (*Bus 3a, 3b, 23*). It is on the corner of La Profonde Rue (B31) and La Rue de Diélament, after Trinity church travelling east.

Coming to **Augrès Manor** is a double treat, because there are the interesting architectural details to enjoy as well as the fascinating animals to watch. The main part of the manor itself dates back to the eighteenth-century, as can be seen by its balanced proportions and the gable stone with a carved face dated 1795. The east-facing wing, with its arch and several blocked windows, could be all that remains of the front of an earlier manor house.

The Manor is set in 31 acres (12.5 hectares) of parkland and here in their family groups are to be seen over 100 species of endangered animals. They do not make up just another 'zoo' but are part of a unique sanctuary where colonies of threatened species have been established and built up into reservoirs against extinction. As the breeding groups have grown since the setting up of the Wildlife Preservation Trust in 1963, some have been returned to their original habitat, such as the pink pigeons hatched in captivity and set free in their native Mauritius. Others have been sent to similarly conservation-minded zoos to help with an overall breeding plan for endangered species.

Among the birds most popular with visitors are the parrots, the showy Palawan peacock pheasants, and the elegant, pink-tinted Chilean flamingoes. Most of the larger birds have their own special areas where they are free to live as they would in the wild, such as the

An orang-utan at the Jersey Zoo.

serious-looking white-naped cranes who dig in the turf for root tubers and seeds in one of the marshier parts of the manor grounds.

Then there are the strange-looking fruit bats, the appealing lemurs, including the ringtailed and the black-and-white ruffed varieties, the aye-ayes which can only be seen in Jersey Zoo, or the different types of monkeys, including pied, emperor and black-lion tamarin. The golden-lion tamarin and the silvery marmosets live freely in the woodland.

The larger primates, such as the apes, orang-utans and the gorillas all have their special and separate breeding and play areas where they can be seen with their families without any danger to the public. The animals that most visitors want to watch and photograph are the gorillas in their half-acre (0.2 hectare) complex.

There is an admission charge to the zoo, but there is a shop before the entrance where visitors are free to browse round the enormous range of items for sale, from animal prints, ornaments and fluffy toys to jigsaw puzzles, stationery and books, including all the well-loved titles by Gerald Durrell, including *My Family and Other Animals*. There is a guide to the zoo on sale at the entrance, for those who want more background information about the reptiles, birds and animals on show.

Jersey Zoo is an ideal place for the whole family to visit, for not only is there a special playground for the children, where they can imitate the athletic antics of the gorillas and orang-utans nearby, but also the Dodo Restaurant where everyone can relax over a cup of tea or light refreshments. As the grounds are so vast, you can see just as little or as much as you want to in newly wooded parkland in a beautiful part of the island. Disabled visitors are welcome and anyone wishing to further the work of the Durrell Wildlife Conservation Trust, which is registered as a charity in both Jersey and the UK, can become a member.

Above: The Eric Young Orchid Foundation.

Other Places of Interest in Trinity

Trinity has benefited not just from the abiding passion of one of its residents but two. So just as the late Gerald Durrell's youthful enthusiasm for all living creatures has led to Jersey Zoo, so the late Eric Young's enthusiasm for orchids has led to the setting up of **The Eric Young Orchid Foundation** (*Bus 21 to Victoria Village*).

Eric Young was born in 1911 in Derbyshire and his passion for orchids began in his early teens when he was shown two orchid plants by the family gardener. When he arrived in Jersey after World War II, Eric Young bought a rundown market garden in Mont Millais, St Helier, and stocked it with the plants from an old orchid nursery in England that was closing down – so came about the nucleus of the superb collection that has been growing in quality and renown ever since.

During the 1970s, Eric Young's work with orchids gained him such prestigious positions as Chairman of the World Orchid Conference Committee and membership of the Research Committee of the American Orchid Society, of which he was also appointed an Honorary Judge. In 1982, in the RHS British Orchid Growers' Association Show, his exhibition was awarded a Gold Medal for its quality of plants and standard of cultivation.

There was still a dream to be fulfilled, however. Eric Young wanted to set up a foundation to maintain the collection and continue his work in perpetuity. A suitable place was eventually found – on the site of a derelict tomato nursery in Victoria Village, Trinity. Sadly, Eric Young died before his dream could be fully realised, but the Foundation has now become a popular venue for visitors.

To get to the Orchid Foundation from St Helier, take the Trinity Road to the Town Mills and then follow the road through Les Grands Vaux, with the reservoir on the left. Continue up Le Mont de la Rosière and on through Victoria Village, turning left at the sign for the Orchid Foundation. Coming from any other part of the island make for Victoria Village and turn down the road on the south side of Victoria Stores, La Rue du Moulin du Ponterrin.

The whole environment of the Foundation complex is ideal – landscaped gardens in a typical part of rural Jersey at its best. There is also a large car park. The display area inside is enhanced by hundreds of orchids. There is also a viewing gallery on a high level where visitors can observe the work of the foundation.

In the display area, look for the white Sobralia from South America; the bright red spray of the Peruvian Cochlioda Noetzliana; the green flowers of the coolly elegant Lycaste Guinevere and the delicacy of the miniature Cymbidium, bred in Jersey and remembering in its name both an island beach and Eric Young's first nursery in St Helier – Cymbidium Petit Port 'Mont Millais'. The founder himself is commemorated in one of the Foundation's fine breeding lines, the mainly yellow Odontioda Eric Young.

The excellent work done at this Jersey orchid centre, and the superior quality of the plants it produces, is shown by the top awards it has been awarded at World Orchid Conferences.

Places to Visit

Eric Young Orchid Foundation

Victoria Village, Trinity

☎ 01534 861963

www.ericyoungorchidfoundation.co.uk

Open: Feb–Dec, Wed–Sat, 10am–4pm. Disabled access.

The Old Forge

Route d'Ebenezer, Trinity

☎ 01534 862637

See wrought-iron work.

Open: weekdays from 8am–5pm (4.30pm on Fridays).

Jersey Zoo (Durrell Wildlife Conservation Trust)

Les Augrès Manor, Trinity

☎ 01534 860000

www.durell.org

Open: daily 9.30am–6.pm. Winter: 9.30am–5pm. Closed Christmas Day. Admission charge. Disabled access.

Mont Orgueil Castle

Gorey, St Martin

☎ 01534 633375

www.jerseyheritage.org

Open: daily summer 10am-6pm, winter 10am–till dusk. Admission charge includes museum of archaeology. Reduced admission charge for senior citizens and students; children under 6 free.

Pallot Steam Museum

Rue de Bechet, Trinity

☎ 01534 865307

www.pallotmuseum.co.uk

Open: 1 Apr to 31 Oct, Mon–Sat 10am–5pm. Railway rides. Tue and Thu mid-June to mid-Sept; Thurs only other times.

Rozel Manor

Off La Grande Route de Rozel, St Martin

Open for special events only.

4. St John and St Lawrence

Around St John

As the parish of St John has probably one of the finest coastlines on the island, visitors will want to see it for themselves straight away. It extends from Giffard Bay, on the edge of Trinity, westwards to Mourier Valley, where the parish of St Mary begins, and from its headlands on a fine day the other Channel Islands and the Cotentin Peninsula can be seen.

The St John Coastline

Jersey's north coast is quite unlike any of the other island coastlines, perhaps with its sheer cliffs dropping to the tumultuous seas below more resembling Cornwall. There are, though, several sheltered bays along its length, and in St John is the truly delightful **Bonne Nuit Bay** (*Bus 4*), protected by the cliffs which reach round to La Crête to the east and Frémont Point to the west.

Les Nouvelles Charrières (C98), as it bends down to the bay, gives glimpses of the sea through the trees before it comes to the tiny harbour of Bonne Nuit itself. The cliffs towering over 400ft (120m) above it are covered with purple heather in the summer, contrasting with, near where the few houses are perched, cascades of pink roses. The small beach extends at low tide to the end of the pier, revealing a long stretch of yellow sand, but swimmers should remember that when the tide is out, the beach shelves quite quickly into deep water. Otherwise bathing in the harbour area is quite safe.

The small pier was constructed in 1872 and the wooden huts on it are for the use of fishermen who can often be seen unloading their catch of lobsters and crabs. Early on a Saturday, local shoppers come here to buy their weekend seafood. The pier too affords a peaceful spot for angling.

Bonne Nuit is also the finishing point for the annual Sark to Jersey Rowing Race which is held in July. When the race was first rowed, in 1967, the time taken used to be anything from 4–7 hours to get all the competitors in. Now the first rowers are back in about 2½ hours. It is an exciting race to watch.

To the right of Bonne Nuit Bay is one of the fortifications put up by the British from 1736 to the mid-nineteenth-century against a possible French attack. This fort, constructed at La Crête point in 1835, is now the weekend and holiday residence of the Lieutenant-Governor.

Earlier fortifications included a boulevard for two cannons, a guardhouse and a powder magazine. In the nineteenth-century even a barracks was built. Yet, for all the money the States poured into these defences at Bonne Nuit, the French never attempted to land here. What did take place, however, was a great deal of smuggling, of which this confession of the *Eliza*'s captain is only one example:

'Instead of proceeding to St Germain, for which we had cleared, we went to Bonne Nuit, and took in 2½ tons of tobacco, spirits in casks, cigars, and snuff, which I agreed to take to Wales at the rate of £50 per ton. We proceeded to Fishguard, where we arrived on the fifth day, and, running in about eleven that evening, assisted in conveying the goods to a store close by. We then went to St Germain, took in 32 sheep, and returned to Jersey.'

To complete the picture of Bonne Nuit there is a harbourside café, decorated with hanging flower baskets, for souvenirs, beach requirements and light refreshments. It is open from

9am–5pm in the summer; winter opening times may vary. Toilet facilities are just a few yards away along the road. ☎ 01534 861656

Bonne Nuit is certainly the spot to put visitors into a holiday mood. Walkers, too, will be pleased to find it an excellent starting point for three different walks. To the east there is the 4-mile (6.5km) walk along the cliff path to Bouley Bay, while to the west there is the shorter walk to La Saline. These cliff walks are quite strenuous and sensible shoes should be worn. The number 4 bus will take walkers back to Bonne Nuit or to St Helier. A shorter circular walk can be taken on National Trust property on the hillside overlooking the bay, on the south side of the C98.

Rounding Frémont Point and going west, the next place to visit is the **Wolf's Caves** 400ft (122m) down a steep and winding path of 307 steps. There is a warning at the top: first to check the tides and, secondly, that the steep climb back is not for the faint-hearted. For those who do go there is a cave 350ft (107m) long, 60ft (18m) high and at its widest 50ft (15m) wide.

Continuing round the coast one is rather unpleasantly reminded that St John is the parish famous for its granite quarries. **Mont Mado quarry**, just north of the B63, was once the most famous. One of the uprights in Grouville's La Hougue Bie dolmen was brought from here; centuries later the States always demanded Mont Mado granite – renowned for its beautiful rose colour – for their official buildings, while the wealthiest families had their houses, if not entirely made of, at least faced with Mont Mado granite. Jersey's main

quarry today, though, is **Ronez quarry**, on Ronez Point, looking eastwards over Mourier Bay and westwards over La Houle. It is an unwelcome intrusion, with its conveyor belts and noisy lorries, into the peace of the St John country-side, but, looking back from Sorel Point at its dusty quarried terraces, there is a certain fascination in watching Jersey's famous granite being hacked out of the ground.

Sorel Point, the next headland along the coast, is the island's most northerly spot. From here to the west can be seen the treacherous Paternoster reef and beyond that, Sark, while to the east can be seen the Normandy coast. At its tip is a lighthouse and inland, to the left a cliff path, leading to Grève de Lecq, past Mourier Valley and Devil's Hole, in the parish of St Mary. Sorel Point can be reached by joining the same cliff path at Bonne Nuit, or Wolf's Caves, or by driving west along La Route du Nord and looking for the turning on the right which is well signposted. There is a motocross track on the Sorel headland where about eight meetings are held between March and May, in September and at the beginning of October. Anyone wishing for further details should see the local press.

Leaving the cliff tops for a moment, between Ronez and Sorel, when the tide is halfway, it reveals in the cliffs a rect-angular hollow, 15ft (4.5m) deep which measures 25ft (7.5m) by 24ft (7m). Such an unexpected shape at such an inac-cessible spot obviously led islanders to speculate on its purpose. So they decided it was there for the fairy folk to bathe in and called it **Lavoir des Dames!**

The cliff path continues from Sorel

Point into **Mourier Valley** (*no bus*), perhaps one of the most isolated spots in Jersey. At the sea end there are plenty of quiet spots among the rocks for a picnic and for a tranquil view of the St Mary coastline. There is also an inland path which leads to the waterworks pumping station and eventually into the parish of St Mary. This is very much a get-away-from-it-all spot, ideal for the self-sufficient walker or rambler. Car drivers can continue west along La Rue de Sorel and Le Mont de la Barcelone and then turn right up Le Chemin des Hougues to reach the footpath into Mourier Valley.

The road which has made this coastal strip accessible to the public, La Route du Nord, was built comparatively recently – during the German Occupation. Even before the war, islanders depended heavily on the tourist trade for their employment but, once the Germans had landed in June 1940, tourist employees were immediately without a job, leaving the Labour Department the task of finding work for over 2,000 people. Then it was decided to use this redundant workforce to build a road along the north coast, largely across private land, that would not help the German war effort, but would be of benefit to the island. La Saline was the starting point and the road makers managed to get as far as Sorel, but then were prevented from getting to Les Mouriers, their original target, because the Germans designated the area between Sorel and Les Mouriers a military zone, to which no access by islanders was possible. After the Occupation, however, La Route du Nord was completed and the period of its first miles of construction is remembered in the dedication which can be seen in the car park off the road opposite Les Fontaines Tavern just before Ronez Quarry. 'This road is dedicated to the men and women of Jersey who suffered in the World War, 1939–1945'.

Walking the Coastline

The main activity to be enjoyed in St John's parish, is, of course, to walk that magnificent coastline. That there is this footpath network round the island's coasts is due to the hard work of those who were on the States' job creation scheme, which operated during the winter for those who would otherwise be unemployed, together with the efforts of the National Trust and conservation volunteers, plus the co-operation of the many landowners involved.

It should be remembered, however, that this is a cliff path and walkers would be well advised for both comfort and safety to wear a pair of stout shoes. It could also be dangerous, or a question of trespassing on private property, to leave the official footpath. Finally, as parts of this north coast path are strenuous, they may be too much for the elderly or unfit. For those who want a good walk, the starting point in this parish going west to Grosnez (8 miles (13km)) or east to Rozel (6 miles (9.5km)) is Bonne Nuit, on the number 4 bus route. At Bonne Nuit itself, on the hillside facing the bay, is an easier, shorter and circular walk, well signposted.

Inland St John

As well as having such a spectacular stretch of coastline, St John also has

Wildlife Paradise

The north coast is also ideal for all birdwatchers and lovers of wild flowers. From the cliff paths, far out to sea, gannets from the nearby colony at Alderney can sometimes be seen feeding. Closer to shore are the puffins and razorbills and the best times to spot them are early morning or evening. On the rocky cliff ledges the herring gull, fulmar petrel and the glossy black shag lay their eggs, while those parts of the cliffs which are densely covered by gorse are ideal hiding places for the shy Dartford warbler. Often soaring overhead is the island's only resident falcon, the kestrel.

A joyful sight in spring is the wild daffodils, known as lent-lilies, pushing their way up through the dead brown bracken, on many a cliff slope. Other flowers to colour these cliff tops are yellow gorse, purple heather, pink foxgloves and campion, blue sheep's bit (rather like scabious) and white ox daisies.

Walking the north coast and (inset right) Gorse.

within its boundaries the stone which is meant to mark the island's centre. This is to be found on the left-hand side of La Rue des Servais, the road which branches to the left along La Grande Route de St Jean (A9), just after the large Sion Methodist Church. The stone itself would not appear to be a local one but could have been part of the now lost dolmen at La Hougue Brune. In any event, the stone is prehistoric.

In this area of **Sion** (*Bus 5*), there are several places of interest. There is the **Methodist church** built to serve the growing band of Methodists in the country parishes. On the other side of the road, a little to the north and making the corner of La Grande Route de St Jean (A9) and Des Houguettes, is another nonconformist landmark. This is **Macpéla cemetery**, which served as the burial place for non-Anglicans when, in the early nineteenth-century, only Anglican clergymen were allowed to officiate at funerals in the parish church cemeteries. It was, therefore, much used by the refugee population who flocked to Jersey after the European upheavals in 1848. The man who often marched behind the red flag in the funeral procession and then delivered the funeral oration at the death of one of the exiles, during his own exile in Jersey, was Victor Hugo. Finally, there is also a useful general stores in this central part of the island and a large DIY centre to browse round, northwards up La Grande Route de St Jean.

St John's Village and the Surrounding Area

Leaving La Grande Route de St Jean, which has along its length so many pink granite walls and traditional arches, take the left turn at Hautes Croix, the continuation of the A9, for St John's Village (*Bus 5*). Just beyond the intersection of the A9 and A10 are the four essentials of any village – the church, the school, the Parish Hall and a pub. A new housing estate, including a chemist and general store, clusters discreetly round the north side of the church. There is also a children's playground, given to the parish by the holiday camp pioneer, Sir Billy Butlin, who retired to Jersey and lived in St John.

As with all Jersey churches, **St John's parish church** (*Bus 5*) has grown over the centuries. The chancel, with its high roof and rough stones, is in essence the original tiny church. As the population of the parish increased, the west wall of this early chapel was pulled down in order that the present nave could be built. At the end of the fifteenth-century, the south aisle, the tower and the spire were added. The church has been the centre of parish worship for over 800 years and its list of known rectors goes back to the thirteenth-century.

Relics of the island's past are still to be seen, both outside and inside the church. Outside is the base of a wayside cross, dating back to the fifteenth-century; inside, the reredos of the Lady Chapel has the Ten Commandments, the Creed and the Lord's Prayer written in French, reminding today's worshippers that a French version of the Book of Common Prayer was used in all the parish churches

111

right up until the early twentieth-century. The chandeliers that hang from the roof of the church are the original oil-burning lamps, wired for electricity as recently as 1935. The rose window, high in the west gable, is specially worthy of note for the vividness of its primary colours which convey the vital energy of the Holy Spirit's gifts – the subject depicted. Then there is St John's distinctive cross, delicately engraved on the glass of the main doors.

St John's *perquage*, the path by which criminals who had taken sanctuary in the church were allowed to escape to the sea, is not a direct one to the nearest harbour of Bonne Nuit as one would imagine. Instead the path crosses the whole of the island to St Aubin's Bay in the south, so that the criminal could have calmer waters when he sailed to his exile. After going through the garden of a house called Les Buttes, it then followed the course of the stream, until it met up with St Mary's *perquage* near Gigoulande Mill. From here it went down St Peter's Valley to Tesson Mill, where it joined St Lawrence's *perquage*. The last section of St John's *perquage* crossed Goose Green Marsh and came out on the shore between Beaumont and Bel Royal. A long last trek across his native island for any criminal about to be outlawed forever from it.

The ornate tomb of Sir Billy Butlin – the well-known holiday camp millionaire and philanthropist who lived in St John – with its inscription containing 2,000 letters, can be seen in the cemetery, 300yd (270m) west of the church along the main road.

For those keen on indoor sports the answer is **St John's Sports and Recreation Centre** (*Bus 5*) in St John's Village, whose extension, the Sir Billy Butlin Memorial Hall, was opened by the Duke of Edinburgh in 1983. Any visitor who wants to sample the sports on offer has to obtain a temporary membership card. Here there is indoor and outdoor tennis, squash, badminton, snooker, short bowls and a shooting range. There is a bar overlooking the cricket pitch and football field.

A little to the east of the village centre is an attraction which is proving very popular. It is on La Route des Issues, has a large car park and is called **Jersey Goldsmiths Lion Park** (*Bus 5*), where the visitor can not only watch craftsmen fashioning the gold but also browse at leisure round the largest selection of gold items on display in the whole of the Channel Islands.

There is an air of opulence as soon as the visitor walks into the open-plan display centre. At one end is Bergerac's shining red car, for followers of the TV *Bergerac* series to admire, and there is also another, an Aston Martin DB7, complete with all its gadgets, on display in the showroom. The memorabilia collection features items owned and worn by Marilyn Monroe and Elizabeth Taylor.

There is the opportunity to buy anything here, at one of the many showcases, from a simple gold chain, cut to any length required, to a gold Swiss watch. There are also complete sets of matching jewellery on view and commissions to make any special item are willingly undertaken. As well as the making of up-to-the-minute fashion jewellery, alterations can be done on the premises. And there is the fascination of watching the craftsmen at their intricate task.

There is also the Gold Café, where food and drink can be enjoyed either indoors or outdoors.

And what an ideal setting the Gold Centre is for spending a couple of leisurely hours, for the colour of the beautifully laid out gardens including a treasure trail and play area for children.

Not much of prehistoric times survives in the parish of St John but it does have one of the few inland dolmens. This is **La Hougue Boëte**, just north of St John's Manor. The mound shows what the monument looked like after it had been sealed. The remains that were found in the burial chamber show that at least one human and several horses were buried here. Though the closed chamber dating back to 3800–2000BC is on private land, it has an interesting link with more modern times. It was used as the meeting place for the seigneurial court of the fief in which the mound stood. There are several other instances in the island where a prehistoric site, because it has been hallowed by past centuries' worshippers, has been used in this way, thousands of years later.

La Hougue Boëte Manor, which is now known as **St John's Manor**, is architecturally one of the island's most impressive houses. It is not known, unfortunately, when it was transformed from the traditionally seventeenth-century Jersey house it once was to the fine classically proportioned one it now is. Nevertheless, it has been called 'The Blenheim of the Channel Islands', and, when it was sold in 1874, had in its grounds not only a cricket pitch but also a croquet lawn, an archery ground, a rifle range and a gravel pit. With the manor, in those pew-paying days, went three pews in St John's church. The house and gardens are closed to the public, except for occasional charity events, but any passer-by can enjoy the colourful displays of flowers that mark both entrances to the manor.

A further activity to enjoy in St John's parish is horse riding. *Le Claire Riding Stables* is on La Rue Militaire (*Bus 4, 5, Hautes Croix*) ☎ 01534 862823 and both riding lessons and hacking are available here. Any visitor who has come without the necessary gear but who fancies a ride through the leafy lanes of St John will be provided with a hat without extra charge.

St Lawrence

This central parish of St Lawrence is bounded by brooks and renowned for its water, its walks, the benefactions of Florence Boot, its Underground Hospital and the island's first woman Constable. On its southern side it has a mile or so of coastline along St Aubin's Bay from Millbrook to Beaumont. Its eastern boundary runs up along Waterworks Valley and its south-western limit starts at the brook just east of Beaumont. Its northern boundary is about 1.5 miles (2.5km) from St John's north coast. The prefix 'Coin' in the parish simply means 'district' and applies to four of the six vingtaines into which the parish is divided.

Waterworks Valley

The parish's chief glory is what used to be called St Lawrence Valley. This runs the whole length down Le Chemin des

Moulins and today it is better known, rather prosaically, as Waterworks Valley (*Bus 7, to St Lawrence's church*). Centrally positioned of Jersey's five picturesque valleys which run from north to south across the island, its swiftly flowing stream of 3 miles (4.75km) long once powered no fewer than six watermills – hence the stream's name, Mill Brook. Right up until the mid-nineteenth-century four of these watermills were part of Jersey's milling industry. The wheat was bought in Russia, carried to the island tax-free in Jersey boats, ground here into flour and then exported, mostly to the colonies. This lucrative trade only came to an end with the introduction of the faster and more powerful steam flour mills. The other two mills in St Lawrence Valley were used for paper making and crushing sugar cane.

That the watermills were no longer needed did not mean an end to the harnessing of the plentiful supply of water in St Lawrence Valley. With the large increase in population of St Helier in the 1880s, supplying the town with fresh water was a problem for which the system of street pumps which already existed proved quite inadequate. So, in 1863, a waterworks company was formed which decided to utilise the water in St Lawrence.

The venture, excellent though it was in principle, in practice proved a disaster and the company went bankrupt. Then, in 1882, a second enterprise, calling itself the New Waterworks Company, built three new reservoirs over a period of 40 years: Millbrook in 1892, Dannemarche in 1908 and finally, in 1929, on the site of an old china clay quarry, Handois. It is no wonder then, that the charm that these man-made and interconnecting lakes have given to the valley should lead to it now being called Waterworks Valley.

Walking in St Lawrence

St Lawrence is the parish for rural walking. And not just along the half-mile (0.8km) which is thought to be, though there is no conclusive proof, all that is left of St Lawrence's *perquage* from the church to the sea. This short walk starts at the southern end of St Peter's Valley, goes through Goose Green where the Seigneur of Hambye slew the dragon and comes out on La Route de La Haule in St Aubin's Bay.

Parishioners and volunteers undertook a Millennium Project to build a new Parish Walk. It stretches from just below Handois Reservoir in the north to the bottom of La Ruelle de St Clair in the south. As it is a woodland walk appropriate footwear should be worn. It is not suitable for people with disabilities or wheelchair users. It takes approximately 1¼ hours at an average pace to cover the walk in one direction. Information about the path, those who built it and the flora and fauna of the valley can be found on the information board where the path passes near Vicart.

Millbrook

The Boot family have strong associations with St Lawrence just as the Butlin family have with St John. Both have been equally generous benefactors to their adopted island home. Jesse Boot, the famous chemist, and his wife Florence

*Glass Church,
St Matthew's*

lived in Villa Millbrook which is up La Rue de Haut off the St Aubin's Inner Road in Millbrook (*Bus 7, 8, 8a, 9, 12, 12a, 15*). The site was first built on by a privateer in 1704 and when this house was demolished another was built in neoclassical style around about 1880. When this was bought by Sir Jesse Boot in 1924, it was first called Lansdowne and then Springland. Today it is known as Millbrook Manor.

Just over the road from the Manor, on the south side of St Aubin's Inner Road, are two examples of the generosity of Sir Jesse Boot's wife Florence, Lady Trent, after he died. The first is **St Matthew's, the Glass Church**. This was originally built as a chapel of ease in 1840, to serve people who, despite the sand dunes which lay between what is now

Victoria Avenue and the Inner Road, began to settle in the Millbrook area, then considered 'one of the prettiest of Jersey villages'. These new parishioners found it too much of a climb to walk or ride on horseback up to St Lawrence's parish church for services.

The resulting chapel was a very plain building and on the death of her husband, Lady Trent decided to beautify

Waterworks Valley.

its interior in memory of him. As well as an architect to help her, she asked the famous glass worker René Lalique of Paris to contribute his considerable talent.

Monsieur Lalique's unique glass work starts at the main doors – in the panels of the doors are two angels. Once inside, the church is dominated at the bottom of the main aisle by the great cross behind the altar flanked by two pillars, all three illuminated. The altar of the Lady Chapel to the left is decorated by a striking quartet of angels.

Once the visitor has gained an overall impression, there are smaller details to notice. A recurring image is that of the lily, a symbol of purity, so that both the Madonna lily and Jersey's own lily can be seen on the screens and the windows. On the glass font – probably the only one in existence – the signature 'R. Lalique' can be seen at the base.

Lalique's work is austere and executed in plain glass, so the visitor should not expect the effect of stained glass. The attraction of this glass is its form and shape and, above all, its luminescence. It is no wonder, therefore, that so many people come to see the uniqueness of the 'Glass Church', as it is so often called, for themselves.

In the vestibule, as well as religious books there are cards, leaflets and transparencies of the church and its glass.

Three years after the rededication of St Matthew's church, Lady Florence Trent had laid out an extensive garden in Millbrook, where once there had just been scrubland. Lady Trent gave it to the island in 1937 on condition that it was always kept as a place where the young could play and the old could rest. As this was the year in which King George VI and Queen Elizabeth were crowned, it is known as **Coronation Park** (*Bus as for Millbrook*).

This is an ideal spot for parents who want to sit and children who want to play. Near the Inner Road entrance there is a children's paddling pool as well as a playground, full of modern as well as traditional equipment, including a steam roller to scramble over and pretend to steer.

Close to the Victoria Avenue entrance is a wide pavilion, with a view of the colourful gardens and then St Aubin's Bay beyond. At this end there is also a venture playground, specially built for the use of people with disabilities, which others enjoy trying their climbing skills on too. There is a refreshment kiosk in the grounds as well as toilet facilities.

To complete this area of interest at Millbrook, there is a group of shops to the east of La Rue du Galet including a supermarket and a post office.

Prehistoric Remains

There are not as many remnants of the past for the public to see in this parish as there are in some others. From prehistory, two great blocks of granite from some dolmen on Mont Félard and a large block of red granite, where the parishes of St Lawrence, St Peter and St Mary meet, called Pierre des Baissières, are all that remain of the menhirs. Specimens from the Bronze Age hoard of axes, knives and other implements that were dug up in an orchard on the Mainlands estate are on view at La Hougue Bie Museum.

Around the Parish

The church, the Parish Hall, the parish arsenal and the school come one after the other along La Grande Route de St Laurent, one of the major roads running north–south through St Lawrence. The oldest of these is **St Lawrence's parish church** (*Bus* 7,), which started off as a chapel and was consecrated as a church on 4 January 1199. One remnant of the earliest church on this site is a broken granite pillar – not of Channel Island origin – now displayed in the south porch. Originally it belonged, apparently, to a fourth-century Roman building. Then, in about the sixth-century, its flat top was inscribed with letters suggesting a Christian memorial to a priest, though no one now knows its meaning. Two or three centuries later, an embellished Anglo-Celtic interlaced pattern was carved down one side. In the south porch itself, which was a chantry chapel in Norman times, a plain brass cross marks the recess in the wall where the tabernacle holding the blessed sacrament was probably kept. The few fragments of medieval glass that survived the Calvinist régime can be seen in the small window above the west door.

Later alterations and additions include, in 1524, the fine Hamptonne Chapel, with its vaulted roof – unique in Jersey – and grotesque gargoyles, representing the spirits of evil driven out by the worship of the congregation. This chapel is probably the finest example of church architecture anywhere in the island. The church bell, dated 1592, is the oldest in Jersey and is still used.

The three south chancel windows portray the story of St Lawrence and his martyrdom by being roasted alive on a grid. It is this grid which has been taken as the parish emblem. The church has been called, because of its size and its fine architecture, 'The Cathedral of Jersey'.

Other glimpses of the island's past can be seen in its old manors, of which **Hamptonne** – perhaps the finest and most interesting house in the parish – is now open to the public as a fascinating country life museum. There is a car park here, but for those coming by bus it is a 10-minute walk from Three Oaks (*Bus* 7,).

The earliest recorded owners of the farm were the Langlois family. The house that Richard Langlois owned in the fifteenth-century was simply one large room, open to the roof, in which the whole family would have lived and slept. Across the road from the house is the unusual square *colombier* or dovecote, that he was allowed to build in 1445 – a rare privilege then – in recognition of his status in Jersey.

A century later, a first-floor hall was added over the ground-floor room and when Laurens Hamptonne acquired the property in the seventeenth-century, there was a further extension – this time two storeys at the east end of the house. This is what visitors to Hamptonne see today – the property restored to the thatched farm with its pillared porch that Laurens, his wife Philippine and his four children lived in over three hundred years ago.

Over the open fire downstairs hangs the *trepis* or cauldron in which the family meals would have been cooked; upstairs is a replica of the curtained four-poster

Hamptonne Country Life Museum.

bed in which Laurens and his wife would have slept, as well as truckle beds for their children. Both downstairs and up are the great chests where the family kept their clothes. In each room where these objects are set out, as if waiting for the family to return, there are booklets explaining what they are and how they were used.

The Langlois House shows eighteenth-century living conditions, with stalls for farm animals downstairs, and living quarters, the equivalent of a 'granny flat', upstairs.

The next building is the Syrvets' house, dating from 1830, with an exhibition called 'Living Memories'. This includes a 12-minute video with archive film and interviews with island residents, and shows how farming has changed in Jersey over the last seventy years.

There are many attractions at Hamptonne, including a nature walk, daily guided tours and demonstrations, a restaurant offering island dishes; and a small collection of farm animals and poultry.

Les Saints Germaines and Avranches are the other two manors: the first, on the road running from the top of Mont Cochon to Sion, and the second, built in 1818, on the St Lawrence main road at Carrefour Selous, can both be glimpsed from the road. Avranches is set in 50 acres (20 hectares) of ground which were used by the Germans during the Occupation as a secret store for 750,000 gallons of petrol.

Humbler dwellings of interest in the parish, both owned by the National Trust, are Le Rât and Morel Farm (*Bus 7*). These can be reached by taking the first or second turning to the left along La Route de l'Eglise. **Le Rât** is a small cottage, probably built in the seventeenth-century, and is typical of rural housing used by people at that

Le Rât.

time. Nearby, on the opposite side of the road, is La Fontaine de St Martin, whose waters were once thought to have magical properties of healing. Further to the west, along Le Mont Perrine, is **Morel Farm**, the best-known farm in the island. The double roadside arch is perfectly proportioned and probably of an earlier date than the eighteenth-century building which can be seen through it across the cobblestones. Both arches have inscribed keystones: the main arch has '1666 RLG' for Richard Langlois, while the pedestrian arch has 'MLG' for his son, Matthew. By the side of the smaller arch is a mounting block.

This is a working farm, but when he has the time, the present farmer is quite happy to show visitors around the outbuildings and the farm can also be visited on Heritage Open Days. In the bake house the bread oven and the hook for smoking bacon are still in place: in the press house the original cider press and apple crusher are still used late every autumn to transform the apples – with the help of a horse to turn the crushing wheel – into a potent cider.

The attractive inland pocket which includes Le Rât and Morel Farm also features two wooded hillsides or *côtils* both owned by the National Trust. A pleasant walk can be taken from the parish hall, through the woods to make a round trip, via La Fontaine de St Martin and back to La Route de l'Eglise again.

Park the car behind the Parish Hall then walk out of the back entrance of the car park and turn left onto La Route de l'Eglise. Cross the road to a footpath which goes along the side of the house called Abbey Gate. Follow the track down through woodland into the valley and along the bank on the other side. Turn right along the path which goes by Badier Farm. This is one of several fine properties on this walk. It is only a short distance to the road. Turn right onto the road and continue walking through well cultivated farmland. Turn right into the road signed La Rue de la Fontaine de St Martin. On your left pass Morel Farm. The next property is a fine granite farmhouse which also has a mounting block outside – the second in a few hundred yards.

Look for the *abreuvoir* on the left of the road which is a stone trough fed by the valley stream which then flows back through the wall until it crosses the road. Further down on the right is the well, which is called La Fontaine de St Martin. The land on the left belongs to the Jersey National Trust as does the Meadow.

Continue right up Mont l'Evesque and take the first turning right onto La Route de l'Eglise to return to the Parish Hall car park. This is about an hour of easy walking.

Leaving the manors, farm and cottage, the visitor's attention is directed to a notorious relic of a much more recent period in the island's history. It is the **Jersey War Tunnels** (*Bus 8*) built in 1941–4 under the valleys of St Lawrence.

To begin with, the German plan was to have a tunnel as an artillery barracks at Meadowbank to supply the main infantry base at St Peter, together with the island's coastal bunkers. In the next valley of Cap Verd there was to be a gun park. The work of drilling and excavating for these tunnels was too vast for the German army units to undertake alone, so the civilian task force, Organisation

Todt, was brought to Jersey to complete the construction. This workforce, founded by Dr Fritz Todt, was a motley crowd of Spanish Republicans, North Africans, Alsatian Jews, Poles, nationals from occupied France and, from 1942 onwards, several hundred Russian prisoners of war. They were to all intents and purposes slave labour and many of them died in Jersey of harsh treatment, overwork and malnutrition.

The task of blasting the rock face to make the tunnel was also dangerous and it is believed that those who were killed in the frequent rock falls were buried where they fell. To link the tunnels of Meadowbank and Cap Verd involved

excavating 43,900 tons of rock and pouring in about 20,000sq ft (1,800m²) of concrete. But the ambitious underground network was never finished, nor was it ever used as an artillery barracks. After the British invasion of Normandy, when the Germans imagined that the Channel Islands were next to be attacked, the whole complex was turned into a military hospital to cope with the casualties.

So the visitor to the Jersey War Tunnels today will see, recreated down to the last detail, a hospital ward, the operating theatre, a doctor's quarters, the Commandant's office and the important communications centre, just as they were

Morel Farm.

Jersey War Tunnels.

left when Jersey was finally liberated by the British on 9 May 1945: without a drop of blood being shed. Over a kilometre of tunnels are now home to the award winning 'Captive Island' exhibition which presents the islanders' story of the German Occupation of Jersey.

A walk through the woodland site known as the War Trail will reveal remnants of trenches and gun-positions, whilst the Garden of Reflection plays host to a large display of thought-provoking statistics of the Occupation.

For serious researchers there is a Research Centre; you will need to contact the collections manager in advance to book an appointment. Finally in the visitor centre you will find the information desk, shop and café.

Despite having such a small coastline in St Aubin's Bay, St Lawrence's only beach is a very popular one. The beach is sandy but kept clean by the tide; the bathing is quite safe at both high and low tide, though there is not much water left to swim in at very low tide; and the whole area is protected by the high sea wall separating the promenade from the beach. On the promenade are both refreshment and toilet facilities all along the bay. Anyone queueing for ice cream at the Old Station Café will be standing

in the place of those who used to queue for tickets for the Jersey Railway that ran between St Helier and St Aubin and on up to Corbière. Millbrook was one of the stops along the line. The other relics of the past along this stretch of the beach are the two German gun emplacements known as resistance nests at Millbrook and Bel Royal. There is an annual sand race in June which is organised by the Jersey Motor Cycle and Light Car Club and it is run at Millbrook. Visitors should see the local press for details.

This parish also provides excellent hacking territory and the place to find a horse is at **Bon Air Stables**, on La Grande Route de St Laurent (A10). Here they not only specialise in children's rides and lessons for novices, but experienced riders are given the thrill of riding along the beach. It should be remembered, however, that from May to the end of September, for the sake of the safety of other beach users, riding on the beach between 10.30am and 6.30pm is prohibited. Riding is by the hour and also takes place on bridle paths along the cliffs. Here at Bon Air Stables everything is taught from jumping to sitting side saddle and proper riding headgear can be borrowed at no extra charge. ☎ 01534 865196

Places to Visit

Glass Church

St Matthew's church, Millbrook,
St Lawrence

☎ 01534 720934

www.glasschurch.org

Open: weekdays 9am–6pm

Hamptonne Country Life Museum

Near St Lawrence church
St Lawrence

☎ 01534 633374

www.jerseyheritage.org

Open: 1 April to 31 Oct, daily 10am–5pm. Reduced admission charge for senior citizens and students; children under 6 free.

Jersey Goldsmiths

Lion Park, St Lawrence

☎ 01534 482098

www.jerseygoldsmiths.com

Open 7 days a week all year from 9.30am–5pm. Free admission. Disabled access.

Jersey War Tunnels

Les Charrières Malorey, St Lawrence

☎ 01534 860808

www.jerseywartunnels.com

Open: Feb to Nov
10am–6pm daily.
Disabled access.

Le Rât

Left off La Route de l'Eglise.

Not open to the public except on Heritage Open days(September).

Millbrook Manor

La Rue de Haut
Millbrook, St Lawrence

Home of Sir Jesse Boot, famous chemist. Not open to the public.

Morel Farm

Along Le Mont Perrine,
St Lawrence

St John's Manor

Near La Hougue Boëte, south of St John's Village

Open for charity functions only.

5. St Mary and St Ouen

St Mary

Inland St Mary

One of the most renowned visitors to the small parish of St Mary was John Wesley. The bicentenary of Wesley's visit here was celebrated in 1987 in Les Marais, where the then 84-year-old founder of Methodism had preached 200 years before. As his Jersey congregation were all French-speaking, Wesley had to address them through an interpreter. John Wesley spent eight days in the island altogether, as part of his Channel Islands tour to meet and preach to the increasing number of his followers.

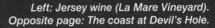

Left: Jersey wine (La Mare Vineyard).
Opposite page: The coast at Devil's Hole.

Methodism, after initial, often violent, opposition, was particularly well received in Jersey as its many large, typically nineteenth-century Methodist chapels bear witness. The Methodist place of worship in St Mary is Bethlehem in Le Haut des Buttes. This was built in 1829 to replace the small chapel which had been erected on a different site 28 years after Wesley's visit.

The original centre of worship in St Mary, though, was **St Mary's parish church** (*Bus* 7), which old documents name as St Mary of the Burnt Monastery. Such evidence as there is, including place names, suggests that this was on or near the site of the present church. How it was burnt down can now only be a matter of conjecture, but it is quite possible that Viking raiders set fire to the monastery. The oldest part of the existing church, now the north-east chancel, dates from the twelfth-century, and if it is the site of the burnt monastery, then people have worshipped there for about a thousand years. A fine chapel was added to the south side of the original chapel in the fourteenth-century. Then, during the Reformation, any relics of its Roman Catholic origins were destroyed, as happened in all the island churches, and the building was transformed into an austere, whitewashed church, frequently described as 'Le Temple'. So it remained until the nineteenth-century, when the old pews, which had been rearranged to face the central pulpit, were replaced by the present pews of Gothenburg pine and part of the south aisle was built on.

Sometime in the island's Christian past, it became a tradition in the three western parishes to ring the church bell all through Christmas Day – without stopping once. The custom probably arose because, during the French occupation of Jersey in the fifteenth-century, St Mary, St Peter and St Ouen were the last to come under the control of the conquerors and the first to be free of them.

The three western parishes still keep up the bell-ringing tradition, although nowadays the bell-ringers do stop while the Christmas services are being held!

St Mary's church gives its name to La Route de Ste Marie and the visitor will be interested to notice the austerity of its interior, the retention of its box pews and the wooden carving of the Annunciation to the left of the main door. The acoustics are good and visitors are welcome to the concerts which are held on some Sunday afternoons in the winter.

St Mary's Coastline

This parish may have the smallest population, under 2,000, but it has the most remarkable stretch of coast (*Bus* 7,) in the island. The 1½ miles (2.5km) of precipitous and frequently indented cliffs from Le Mourier to Grève de Lecq give the visitor a coastal path through gorse and bracken with stunning views, particularly from the promontory called Le Col de la Rocque; caves to marvel at, such as the one that tunnels through L'Ile Agois and the one called the Devil's Hole; and the largest beach on the north coast, Grève de Lecq, although only about one-third of it is in St Mary.

The visitor walking from east to west will probably pick up the coastal path at Sorel in St John and follow it into St Mary up the western slopes of Le Mourier. The stream in this valley used to turn three of the island's watermills, but the water is now diverted to Handois Reservoir in St Lawrence. Once a tranquil haven for the keen walker, Le Mourier is now often the noisy resort of motor scrambling enthusiasts, but from the top of La Plaine to its east and La Falaise to its west, there are spectacular views of the island's north coast in both directions.

From La Falaise the path leads west to the **Devil's Hole** (*Bus* 7), a natural crater in the solid cliff measuring about 100ft (30m) across and plunging 200ft (61m) down. It has been caused by the sea gradually eroding the roof of what was once a cave, until it collapsed and formed a crater. The name 'Devil's Hole' is a dramatic one but was only invented in the nineteenth-century. Formerly it was called 'Le Creux de Vis', 'Le Creux de la Touraille' or Spiral Cave. One possible derivation for its modern name is connected with the shipwreck of a French boat in 1851. Its figurehead was thrust by the tide straight into the hole and someone had the idea of getting a local sculptor to transform the torso into a wooden devil, complete with horns. Today this devil's metal replica stands in a pool on the way down to the crater, to lend atmosphere to the winding – and in one place quite steep – path down to the Devil's Hole itself. The hole can be peered down into from two safe vantage points.

Access to the Devil's Hole is through the grounds of the Priory Inn, which are open all the year round, and is free. Here there are parking and toilet facilities and a wishing well. Lunches are served between 12am and 2pm and there is a gift shop opposite. The Priory can be reached via La Grande Rue or Le Chemin des Hougues for those who are not walking to the Devil's Hole along the cliff path.

After the Devil's Hole, there is the promontory – carpeted in spring with lent lilies and bluebells – owned by the National Trust and known as **Le Col de la Rocque**, where breathtaking views of the cliffs either side can be seen from Plémont Point to Ronez Point. To the north and east all the other islands and the Normandy coast are visible on a clear day. The path then goes on to the cliff above L'Ile Agois, under which is a tunnel. This cave can only be explored at low tide and then only in dry conditions, as the beach is often flooded by the stream which crosses it after heavy rain. **L'Ile Agois** is a 500sq yd (450m²) islet separated from the mainland by a narrow gorge, about 250ft (75m) below the cliffs along which the footpath runs. Evidence in the way of pottery, flint heads and coins suggests that L'Ile Agois was inhabited in Neolithic times and again in the ninth-century AD. As well as blackthorn, primroses and bluebells covering the cliffs here in the spring, wood small-reed (*Calamagostis*), rarely seen in Jersey, grows on the summit of L'Ile Agois.

There is another fine viewing point from **L'Ane**. Beyond this headland the footpath runs further inland south of the rifle and clay pigeon ranges at Crabbé and joins the lane which leads to the most popular beach on the north coast – Grève de Lecq. The walk to here from the Devil's Hole is about 2 miles (3.25km). From Le Câtel there is an almost aerial view of the beach and the densely wooded valley leading to it, with the distinguishing mark of the defence tower – actually in St Ouen – in the car park between the two.

For anyone interested in shooting, **Crabbé's** clay pigeon and rifle ranges can be reached, once you have arrived at St Mary's Parish Hall, by following the signposts to the Crabbé Compost Site, beyond which are the ranges. ☎ 01534 485219

Visitors are welcome to join in the clay pigeon shooting, which includes sporting, skeet, balltrap and down the line shooting, and to enjoy the club facilities. Both guns and tuition by a qualified coach are available. Other shooting here includes the Rifle Association, the Pistol Club and the Smallbore Rifle Club.

La Grève de Lecq

Arriving at Grève de Lecq (*Bus 9*) either by the footpath from Crabbé or down the valley from Le Rondin, the visitor finds more than just the most popular beach on the north coast. First of all, the name 'La Grève' means the beach, and 'Lecq' probably derives from the Norse for a creek. This break in the north cliffs comes at the meeting place of two valleys, to the west from St Ouen and to the east from St Mary. The stream, which flows down the valley from Le Rondin and into the sea through the sea wall, is the dividing line between the two parishes. This means that buildings to the east of Le Mont de Ste Marie, such

as Grève de Lecq Country Apartments, which used to be the married quarters for officers in Napoleonic times, are in St Mary, while those over the road, such as the watermill, known as Le Moulin de Lecq, are in St Ouen.

The whole area of Grève de Lecq is full of historical titbits from the Iron Age to the present day. To begin with the headland to the east of the bay, known as Le Câtel de Lecq (Lecq Castle), the extensive earthworks here were raised to protect the Iron Age inhabitants of Jersey from their enemies. They also served as a refuge for their descendants right down to medieval times.

One of the surviving watermills which ground the flour for these medieval inhabitants still exists. It is **Le Moulin de Lecq** (*Bus 9*) – first mentioned in 1299, standing in meadow and woodland on the way into Grève de Lecq and now converted into an inn. It was in use as a mill right up until 1929, thus serving the area for over 600 years. During the German Occupation, however, the power of the huge 18-ton waterwheel was harnessed for a different purpose – to generate electricity for the searchlights the Germans had positioned round Grève de Lecq Bay. This outside waterwheel, which has a diameter of 21ft (6.5m), works entirely by the weight of the water that rushes past the mill.

Inside the inn, on the ground floor, in the Mill Room, the machinery which worked the mill from inside has been preserved as part of the decor. Upstairs in the bar, where all the grinding took place, one of the mill's old grinding stone sets survives as well as corn-sack style cushions and paraffin lamps.

The Germans were only the last in a

Officer's quarters at Grève de Lecq Barracks.

Grève de Lecq Bay.

long line of defenders of the bay. In fact, such a natural vantage and defence point as Grève de Lecq was used for warlike purposes at several different times over the centuries. The fort overlooking the bay, the battery on the summit of Le Câtel de Lecq and the round tower in what is now the car park were all three built as part of the eighteenth-century defences all round the island against a threatened French invasion.

Further building continued into the next century, with the construction of the **Grève de Lecq Barracks** (*Bus 9*) which have the protection of Le Câtel de Lecq to the north of them They were begun in 1810 at the height of the Napoleonic invasion scare and were com-

Grève de Lecq 'Octopus Pools'

Jersey Towers

To counter the prospect of a French invasion in the eighteenth century, a series of tower fortifications were built around the island. Some were situated offshore, the rest on the coast. The oldest surviving tower is at Grève de Lecq. It was built in 1780 and is 35ft (10.6m) high. It was surmounted by a large cannon mounted on a moveable carriage. Eight of these towers may be seen in the Royal Bay of Grouville and there is a further large tower offshore here.

The Kempt Tower at St Ouen's Bay is later, dating from 1834. It has a much greater diameter and is now a Nature Centre.

The Jersey Tower at Grève de Lecq.

pleted in 1815, the year of Napoleon's defeat at the Battle of Waterloo.

The barracks included rooms for the soldiers, the NCOs and their officers, together with the quarter-master's stores, stables and harness rooms for the horses. The only item in the two tiny whitewashed prison cells was an uncomfortable iron bedstead.

The barracks are now owned by the National Trust for Jersey, and have been fully restored to their original state. As well as the barrack buildings, there is an exhibition of horse-drawn vehicles and an interpretation centre for the natural history of Jersey's north coast.

Also built in the nineteenth century was the pier at Grève de Lecq, which jutted out much further from the western headland than it does now. Thirteen years after it was built, a severe storm broke it up and the granite stones which were strewn across the beach as a result have been used to build a break-water and to repair the stump of pier that remains. Today it makes an ideal place for a bit of fishing and gives, as one looks back, a good view of the beach in its rural setting.

The circle of concrete at the west end of the harbour wall in St Ouen marks one of the many twentieth-century de-fences constructed to guard the bay. It is where the Germans put a tank turret during their nearly 5 years' occupation of the island. On both sides of the bay they also constructed gun emplace-ments. On the eastern side there is the reinforced concrete casemate for a 3-inch (7.5cm) gun and, behind it, a large air-raid shelter; on the western side, the fortress-type concrete casemate housed a 4 inch (10.5cm) gun.

Looking seawards from the beach, the points of a rocky outcrop can be seen around which the white surf breaks. This reef was first called **Les Pierres de Lecq**, and was the scene of a ter-rible shipwreck. In 1565, after Queen Elizabeth I had given Helier de Carteret of St Ouen the authority to colonise the then uninhabited island of Sark, he chose thirty-five Jersey families and five from Guernsey to go with him. Tragically, as the Jersey contingent were crossing the Channel to start their new life in Sark, one of the ships foundered on Les Pierres de Lecq. Among those drowned were women and children and since that day, whenever there is a storm, their terrified cries as their boat first struck the rocks can apparently still be heard. Fishermen call the plaintive sound *'les cris de la mer'* – 'the cries of the sea'.

There are, however, natural as well as historic features to enjoy at Grève de Lecq. Beneath Le Câtel de Lecq there is a cave some 60ft (18m) long, 15ft (4.5m) wide and up to 20ft (6m) high in some places which opens onto the sandy beach of Le Val Rouget to the east. This cave can only be entered when the tide is extremely low and visitors should make quite sure of tide times before venturing to explore it.

The bay itself – most of which is in St Ouen's parish – is popular with families, because of its fine sandy beach and its several cafés and kiosks. It is also shel-tered by the cliffs to the west and east, while the wide expanse of dark, rock-coloured sand is ideal for spreading out on or for ball games. Swimmers should note that the beach shelves steeply into deep water and extra care should be taken if there is a heavy swell. There is ample parking.

For the walker, as well as the 2-mile (3.2 km) cliff path back to the Devil's Hole there is also a further extension of the coastal route westwards. This starts behind the Prince of Wales Hotel and goes along La Charrière Huet, the original track down to the watermill, towards Plémont. From the headland looking back east is the long stretch of the northern cliffs back to Sorel. The bus to Grève de Lecq is the number 9 and for those who want to walk there from either east or west, the number 7 goes to the Devil's Hole and the number 8 to Plémont. There is a return service from all three points to St Helier.

The **La Mare Wine Estate** (*Bus 7 to Devil's Hole*) has a fine house built at the end of the eighteenth-century and is set in several acres of land. It too, though, is not a typically Jersey farm, although a working one. It is, in fact, a vinery which produces two sparkling and two still wines, as well as a grapple, which is a blend of grape and apple wine, and Jersey apple brandy.

This farm is not only beautifully laid out but is practical too, so that one can appreciate to the full all the stages of vine growing and wine-making. There is ample parking and then, just by the admission gate, there is the Vineyard and Orchard Seasons display, which not only gives a brief history of the original farm, but shows the different seasons out in the vineyards and in the orchards.

With this interesting information in mind, the visitor is then free to wander as he or she wishes, or to follow the Vineyard Trail, which is given to each visitor on arrival. This leads through the vineyard itself, round the orchard – and eventually to the building which houses the Vintry, where there is also the distilling of Jersey apple brandy and wine-tasting and the Vineyard Shop. In the Vintry is the charming bow-windowed shop, where there is everything from animal masks, Jersey wine and cider to Jersey mustard, marmalade and preserves – all made in the farm kitchen.

So, although St Mary is a small parish, there is plenty to do there, including walking along its coastline, swimming, surfing and fishing and visiting its two unusual farms. There is magnificent scenery to enjoy as well as historic buildings. La Rue des Buttes (B53) is worth noting, as for any visitors wanting one, there is a handy general store in the forecourt of the garage.

The late-night visitor to Jersey, who comes here after the Battle of Flowers in August, or during early September, will have the extra delight of seeing two National Trust properties floodlit. The first is Grève de Lecq Barracks and the second the headquarters of the National Trust for Jersey, at 'The Elms' farmhouse, on La Chève Rue (A6).

St Ouen

Covering the whole of the north-west corner, St Ouen (pronounced 'wan') is the largest of the island's twelve parishes. Unlike the other eleven, the parish is divided into '*cueillettes*' and not '*vingtaines*', which date back to the time when dues had to be 'gathered' (*cueillir* means to gather) from each of the districts. As about half the parish is still largely uncultivated, consisting of heathland

Produce of La Mare Vineyard.

and sand dunes, and it is surrounded on three sides by the sea, it is not surprising to discover that the whole area is one of outstanding natural beauty.

The Coastal Path

Starting at Grève de Lecq, where the north-east boundary of St Ouen divides the valley, there is a coastal path going west towards Plémont, then continuing above the beach of Grève-au-Lançon and on to Grosnez Castle. This section of the coast is rich in caves and stunning rock formations; it is also an ideal spot for birdwatching. There is a cave in the small and charming bay of Douet de la Mer, the so-called Smuggler's Cove, one further along at Le Grand Becquet and a third at Le Petit Becquet, to mention just a few. As for the birds to be watched, fulmar petrels have colonised the north-facing cliff ledges between Grève de Lecq and Plémont and can mostly be

seen from May to September. Early morning and evening are the best times to catch sight of the breeding puffins and razorbills and the cliffs are often hovered over by kestrel. Looking out to sea, feeding gannets and tern can sometimes be spotted.

The coastal path continues from Grève-au-Lançon and, on the way to Grosnez, passes the archaeologically famous **La Cotte à la Chèvre**, or Goat's Cave, perched several feet above present-day sea level at the west end of Plémont Bay. Recent excavations suggest that man was living here as early as 100,000BC and the flints and coarse stone tools found in the cave area are as important as those Palaeolithic remains found in a cave in St Brelade. These finds are now on display in the museum at La Hougue Bie.

Following the path round the headland one comes to **Grosnez Castle** (*Bus 8*), standing in isolated ruins 200ft (60m) above sea level. The entrance to this north-western refuge is all that is now left standing, but one can still trace where the rest of the walls and buildings would have stood. Carved corbels from the castle are on display in the museum at La Hougue Bie. No records say when the castle was built or how it came to be destroyed – all that is known is that it dates from the fourteenth-century.

There is plenty to see from the headland at Grosnez (which means 'big nose') depending on the weather and the time of day. Bad weather and there will be many passing birds to spot, including the fulmar; a clear day and the other Channel Islands can be distinguished, starting with Guernsey to the north-west, then Jethou, Herm,

Above: the German Battorio Moltke at Les Landes.

Grosnez Castle.

Sark, the Paternosters and, farthest east, Alderney. On a summer evening this is a favourite spot to watch the spectacular sunsets for which St Ouen is renowned. There is parking on the headland for those who want to explore the castle ruins, walk down to the lighthouse, or start walking along the clifftop path that goes south to L'Etacquerel and the start of that magnificent stretch of coastline, St Ouen's Bay.

On the way from Grosnez to L'Etacquerel, one passes the wild open plateau of **Les Landes** (*Bus 8 to Grosnez*), where there are no trees to break the winds that sweep across from the Atlantic Ocean. This is the largest area of continuous heathland in Jersey, with bracken, gorse and dry acidic as well as maritime grassland breaking through the predominantly dwarf scrub heath.

Naturalists might spot the rare Glanville fritillary butterfly, or the Dartford warbler which nests here in quite significant numbers. Just to the north of the Pinnacle Rock, in the wetland area of Le Canal du Squez, is the habitat of the equally uncommon and protected agile frog. In this bogland thrive purple moorgrass, St John's wort and the bog pimpernel. Casual walkers will notice, on the outcrops of rock, natural rock gardens with white sea campion, pink thrift and the pale yellow spikes of the pennywort, while, in the spring, almost underfoot is the lilac sand crocus in the turf and all about, the unmistakable fragrance of the gorse.

In the extreme north of Les Landes, to the west of Le Chemin du Château which leads to Grosnez Castle and La Mare Route de Grosnez, is the island's one mile (1.6km)-round race course. The Jersey Race Club hold about nine meetings here a year, with the first one on Easter Monday and the last on Summer Bank Holiday Monday. Each meeting has five races, including one hurdle race, and starts at 2.30pm including on Sundays. All the races are spaced at 35-minute intervals. All facilities are available at the course and the picturesque setting, together with the thrill of watching the races themselves, makes for a most pleasant afternoon out.

This is also the part of the island where enthusiasts can sail kites and fly model aircraft. Walkers, though, will just wish to wander along the paths through the yellow gorse and purple heather and enjoy the clifftop peace and the views over the sea. From time to time there are reminders of a less peaceful period in the island's history, with the remains of the fortifications that the Germans placed all along this western coast during the island's Occupation: gun emplacements and bunkers still showing through the wild vegetation, together with a concrete observation tower overlooking the Atlantic to the west of the racecourse.

Walkers taking the cliff path from Grosnez to L'Etacq will pass on their right the long slope down to **Le Pinacle** (*Bus 8 to Grosnez*), the almost 200ft (60m) Pinnacle Rock right on the edge of the sea. Despite its exposed position, excavations have revealed that there have been no fewer than five different settlements at its foot, the first dating back to the Neolithic period, the last to Christian times. For there is no doubt that the islanders' veneration of large rocks continued here until about the second-century AD – there are the remains of a pagan shrine to the god of the rock from this period to prove it.

The slope sweeping down to Le Pinacle is a special treat for spring visitors because of the wild flowers that cover it. These include, as well as the expected bluebells, sea pinks with their honey-scented blossoms, creeping broom and the spreading horseshoe vetch – both yellow. Below the rock itself is a cave which is only safe to be explored when the tide is going out – even then extreme care should be taken.

St Ouen's Bay, Les Mielles and the Surrounding Area

Walking south from Le Pinacle, the path descends steeply onto Mont du Vallette at L'Etacq, a huge circular mass of grey rock rising from the beach at the northernmost tip of St Ouen's Bay (*Bus 12a*). Here, right on the shore, an old German bunker has been transformed into a *vivier* where many locals, including restaurateurs, buy their fish. In the large tanks of sea water are live crabs, lobsters, mussels, oysters, clams, whelks and other shellfish. The *vivier* is open 8am–5pm Tuesdays to Saturdays and 8am–1pm on Mondays.

The 5-mile (8km) stretch of the bay and the dunes behind it are divided between the parishes of St Ouen, St Peter and St Brelade. Along St Ouen's part of the bay, known as **Les Mielles** – the island's mini National Park – is **Kempt Tower**. This Martello Tower was built in the first years of the nineteenth-century to defend this part of Jersey's west coast against a possible French invasion. Now it serves as an interpretation centre for the Les Mielles area, its birds, plants and history.

Just opposite Kempt Tower is the Frances Le Sueur Centre, which is the base of the countryside manager rangers. It also serves as an ideal lecture room for such topics as the flora and fauna of the area.

The displays at the interpretation centre have a strong natural history bias, but information can also be found about the area's prehistory. It tells, for example, of a fine example of a passage grave, **Les Monts Grantez** (*Bus 8, 9 to St Ouen's church then walk to Le Chemin des Monts*). This megalithic monument has a rounded, almost polygonal end chamber at the end of a narrow passage. Many of the capstones are still in place, but that over the end chamber was destroyed. Several of these massive stones originate from the southern end of St Ouen's Bay, so the huge effort involved in transporting them to the plateau overlooking the sea would suggest quite a sizeable Neolithic population in the area. The remains found at this prehistoric burial site include the bones of at least 8 people, together with bones of ox, deer, horse, pig and goat. There were also piles of limpet shells, stone artefacts, and coloured pebbles from the beach. The site is surrounded by a granite wall and is on land overlooking the sea owned by the National Trust for Jersey, in direct line with the spire of St Ouen's church.

The sand dunes along this west coast are the ecological focus of Les Mielles and have an extraordinary diversity of plant life. Over 400

St Ouen's Bay.

different species have been recorded growing here, 30 of them locally rare or scarce plants, such as the strange-looking (and smelling) lizard orchid and the great sea stock with its night fragrance. More abundant are the soft fluffy hare's tail grass, often dyed and used on Battle of Flower floats, the tree lupin, with its yellow or white blooms scenting the air from July right through to October, and the prickly bluish green sea holly which has small powder-blue flowers in July and August. At the end of the day, there is the fragrant evening primrose to enjoy.

Dune flora and fauna can be observed along the whole of this coastal strip between the sea wall and the coast road;

some plants, such as the yellow small hare's ear, are so tiny that you have to be on your knees to see them. Here the green lizard, rare in Britain, can be found. Where the sea washes over the wall, the plants found there are more typical of salt marshes. The large mauve blue patches of flowers round Kempt Tower itself are of the Alderney sea lavender, which blooms from June through to August. In fact, there are few times in the year when a plant cannot be seen in flower somewhere in Les Mielles.

Keen ornithologists can get a bird guide from the interpretation centre with a check list to tick off any sighting of the many wild birds that feed and breed in Les Mielles. Many of the birds seen on the dunes, scrub and open grass-land are likely to be permanent residents in Jersey, but any large concentrations of water birds are more likely to be wintering visitors. So that lover of gorse, the stonechat, and Jersey's commonest falcon – actually breeding in St Ouen's Bay – the kestrel, belong here, while the common snipe, which prefers open marshy fields, and the grey heron are only overwintering here. Birds wading along the edge of the sea include the oystercatcher, the dunlin and turnstone, while two regular inland visitors are the wheatear and the yellow wagtail. Bird lovers may like to know that in La Mielle de Morville, beside one of the reed-enclosed ponds, is the RSPB/YOC bird hide, with room for ten, which can be used by members of the public.

The only large, natural, open stretch of water in Jersey is also in St Ouen and a part of the conservation area of Les Mielles. This is La Mare au Seigneur or **St Ouen's Pond** (*Bus 12a*) now owned by the National Trust for Jersey – which is surrounded by extensive reed beds, with sharp rush and great fen sedge on their outer edge, and is therefore an important site for both migrating and overwintering birds.

The Cetti's warbler, with its excited bursts of song, skulks here and during the winter flocks of brent geese can be seen on the pond itself, or in the fields to the east of it. This is the natural habitat too of the breeding coot, moorhen and tufted duck as well as a breeding site for the delicate-looking dragonfly which can be seen anywhere in the summer within Les Mielles.

Also in these wet fields, towards the end of May, grow the uncommon in Jersey, loose-flowered orchids with their tall spikes of rich purple, widely spaced blos-soms, together with several other varieties.

Surfers at St Ouen's Bay.

These orchid meadows are open to the public in May and are well signposted to advertise the fact. Here, too, butterflies can be found, such as the large, small and green veined whites that can be seen throughout the summer and the painted ladies settling on thistles in the area.

Looking west out to sea, you will notice a tower, completely surrounded by water at half-tide. It is a Martello tower, built some time between 1796 and 1800, and given the name Rocco, after the rocky island on which it stands. However, what with the buffeting it got from stormy seas and from the Germans, during the Occupation, using it for target practice, it was in danger in the 1950s of collapsing. Then, in the 1960s, just in time, the tower was restored and La Rocco Tower is now one of the landmarks of St Ouen's Bay.

On **St Ouen's Beach** (*Bus 12a*), sand races are held on one or two Saturdays a month throughout the season, and there are ¼-mile (0.4km) standing sprints held on the Five Mile Road just behind the beach. For further details of these events see the local press.

In the water of this, the largest bay in the Channel Islands, one can enjoy swimming, surfing, windsurfing, wave-skiing or catamaran sailing. As the Atlantic ebbs and flows into St Ouen's Bay, swimmers should always obey the instructions of the lifeguards on duty and only swim between the flags. They should also take great care in heavy surf and avoid bathing when the tide reaches the slipways and wall. Non-swimmers should never venture into the surf alone.

Surfing has become one of the island's most popular water sports and in St Ouen's Bay some of the best waves in Europe can be found. Surf and body boards can be hired from several different outlets along the bay, or a full-size board, plus tuition on how to use it, if required. Although most of the wind-surfing is done in the bays of St Aubin, St Brelade and Grouville, some intrepid sailors enjoy the great challenge offered by St Ouen, but use should not be made of an offshore wind. Boards can be hired for those who are competent in surf. It should be noted that the summer months, when the surf is flatter, give perfect conditions for beginners.

There are plenty of free parking areas along the length of St Ouen's Bay, as well as refreshment and toilet facilities, so this is an ideal beach for families to spend a whole day on.

Inland St Ouen

St Ouen has the distinction of having four manor houses. La Brecquette was built in L'Etacq Valley close to the shore and had large forests of oak trees on the east and to the north of it. Then, in 1356, La Brecquette and the forest that surrounded it were, as an early chronicler put it, 'overwhelmed and swallowed up by a terrible hurricane', when 'the sea engulfed a large area of fertile land'. Over 650 years later, when there is an exceptionally low tide, the stumps of the once proud oak forests are still visible, but of the manor there is no sign.

There is a saying in the parish – 'Who says St Ouen says de Carteret.' This is because the de Carteret family have provided a continuous line of Seigneurs of **St Ouen's Manor** (*Bus 9*) for the last 800 years and up to the present day. The Seigneur of St Ouen is the most senior of the island's Seigneurs and his manor is arguably the most historic in the island.

In the twelfth-century the manor house probably resembled more of a castle than a home and from that building only the oldest parts of the two towers remain. The central part of the manor, with its finely proportioned door, dates from the sixteenth-century, while in the seventeenth-century the two wings and a huge kitchen were added.

When Colonel Malet de Carteret inherited the manor in 1856 it had, however, become a ruin and the building visitors see today owes much to his ambitious plans of restoration. He topped the two medieval towers and built a porch onto the main entrance. Inside the manor, with the help of local craftsmen, he created a grand hall, with a staircase and gallery.

In the grounds, de Carteret restored St Anne's chapel, in which the Seigneur and his family would, throughout the Middle Ages, have heard mass daily, but which had been used as a hayloft since the eighteenth-century. Mass is once again held in the restored chapel most Sundays. He also built the lodge and the *colombier* and repaired the imposing avenue to the manor.

During the Occupation of Jersey, 1940–5, the German troops had their quarters in the manor and turned St Anne's chapel into a butcher's shop for the troops, using the altar as a chopping board. They also burnt down the south wing by misusing a stove. This has now been rebuilt.

At Vinchelez are the last two of the parish's four manors – over the road from each other. Travelling west along La Route de Vinchelez, also known as Vinchelez Lane, the manor of **Vinchelez de Bas** is on the right and the manor of **Vinchelez de Haut** is on the left. That there are two manors for the one fief of Vinchelez stems from the fact that in 1607 the fief was divided between two sons. But when it came to claiming possession of the huge whale that was washed up on St Ouen's beach at Le Pulec in 1726, the Seigneur of Vinchelez de Bas' claim won and so, to this day, parts of the jawbones of the huge whale stand at the main road gateway and can be seen from the road. Neither of the two manors, though, is ever open to the public.

Continuing along Vinchelez Lane, said to be one of the island's most picturesque roads, one arrives at Plémont, the headland plateau that overlooks Plémont beach, or Grève-au-Lançon. **Plémont Point** (*Bus 8*), by the way, is an excellent spot for birdwatching: the auk from May to the end of July; the nesting fulmar and shag on the cliffs; linnet, meadow pipit and stonechat in the gorse and bracken.

South from Plémont, along La Route de L'Étacq, is an unusual attraction – **Treasures of the Earth** (*Bus 12a*). Here is a huge cave-like structure in which are exhibited large fossils and minerals, the largest item being a 12.5 million carat amethyst, believed to be the biggest in the world and weighing about 2.5 tons. Everything in the gift shop, too, is made from Mother Earth's treasures, making an unusual souvenir or present.

By the terraces there is a restaurant, where lunches or cream teas can be enjoyed, sitting inside or out, according to the weather. There is also a goldsmith on site, who can be watched as he works.

There is plenty of parking space.

Travelling southward from Plémont along the B56, B34 and A12 down to the centre of the parish, one comes to the main shopping area round the Parish Hall and down the C117 to St Ouen's parish church. Opposite the Parish Hall is a supermarket and a post office. Two special tourist attractions are also here – a pottery and a craft centre.

Bouchet Pottery (*Bus 8, 9*) is behind the Parish Hall and specialises in agateware, a type of marbled pottery. Bouchet Original Agateware has been researched and perfected over 20 years and its originality lies in the fact that the potter making the pottery had a break-through in the mixing of agateware clay, thus producing – with white clay stained with metal oxides – a type of agateware never seen before. Some pieces contain up to eighty shades of colour.

As this process is a carefully guarded secret, visitors cannot actually see the pottery being made, but there is a 12-minute video showing all the processes in making agateware that are not secret.

Above: Bouchet Agateware Pottery.

There is, too, an eye-catching display at the Pottery of all the items made from this unique agateware, from jewellery to ornaments.

St Ouen's parish church (*Bus 8, 9*) is to the west of the A12, La Grande Route de St Ouen, along the C117. When the first church was built in St Ouen is not known, but it is thought that there was a small thatched chantry chapel on the site of the present chancel. St Ouen's church was mentioned in a charter signed by William the Conqueror before he invaded England, so it must have been in existence before 1066.

This same Norman duke had as his most binding oath, 'By St Ouen I swear it', so it is not surprising to learn that the saint to whom the church was dedicated, and whose emblem of a gold cross on a blue ground is the parish crest, was Dadon, the Bishop of Rouen, the capital of William's Normandy. A tiny splinter of the saint's bone is supposed to be built into the main altar.

From the twelfth-century onwards, many enlargements of the church were carried out to accommodate the increasing population, so, for example, a chapel was added in both the thirteenth and fourteenth centuries. Later came the extended nave, the tower and the south and north aisles.

During the sixteenth-century, the church was changed, as were all island churches, into a Huguenot temple, where all the pews were turned to face the central altar at which Holy Communion was celebrated by the whole parish only four times a year. Transformation to an Anglican church came in the nineteenth-century, to which period belong most of the stained glass windows.

Plémont beach. Unfortunately there is a steep descent down to it.

Below: Former German Fort on the north west coast.

St Ouen's is one of the most pictur- esque of the island's parish churches, with its view across the sea from the churchyard. Of special interest to the visitor is the unusual stone staircase leading from the centre of the church to the belfry, the fine seventeenth-century silver plate, and the several memorials to the important de Carteret family – in- cluding their coat of arms in stained glass in the north aisle – whose large railed-in plot in the churchyard is to the right of the entrance gate. The daughter church of St George, built in 1880, is near Portinfer, to the north of the parish.

At the L'Etacq end of the Five Mile Road is another of the craft centres which this north-west corner of the island has seemed to inspire. This is **Jersey Pearl** (*Bus 12a*). Its showrooms hold the largest collection of pearl jewel- lery assembled in the island under one roof. Entrance is free and from the first moment inside Jersey Pearl the visitor will be aware of a feeling of luxury.

As well as pearls being on show, there is an educational display and guided tours available. Then, too, the skills of the craftspeople who make the jewel- lery can be watched as they set rings or thread necklaces. Then there are the well-stocked counters where jewellery with either oyster or crafted pearls can be bought – the range includes necklets and bracelets in single, double or triple rows, rings, earrings, pendants and brooches, in modern or traditional style. The price for an item can be as low as £5 or as much as thousands of pounds, all VAT free. This is certainly the ideal place to buy a piece of pearl jewellery as a holiday souvenir, or to mark a special occasion. You can also have the pleasure of picking your own pearl from an oyster!

To make a visit to Jersey Pearl even more pleasant, there a creperie and ice cream parlour, with breakfast, lunch and Jersey cream teas also on offer.

Nearby is the **Jersey Woollens** shop, selling traditional Channel Island knit- wear, made on the premises, which also sells a range of other clothes and items. On the premises is a unique collection of commemorative pottery and glass bowls, jugs and other items, produced to mark royal occasions since before the war.

Nearby the **Channel Islands Mili- tary Museum** can be found in a coastal bunker overlooking St Ouen's Bay. These items include such fascinating objects as examples of Red Cross Food Parcels; British Liberating Forces' uniforms; internees' mail; and the only collection of military motor cycles in the Channel Islands.

Another must for visitors to St Ouen is the **Battle of Flowers Museum**, off the road that leads from the Parish Hall down to St Ouen's Bay. Here is every Battle float, all prizewinners, entered by Miss Florence Bechelet since 1953. Though only made of dyed hare's tail and marram grass, these floats can depict any scene from the fun of *101 Dalmatians* and the stolid strength of buffaloes on the plain, to the delicate detail of a dovecote, complete with birdseed. The graceful fla- mingoes on the float entitled 'A Bevy of Beauties' are of particular interest, as they were made by Miss Bechelet specially for the Queen's visit to Jersey in June 1978 and then entered for that year's Battle of Flowers in August.

Places to Visit

Battle of Flowers Museum

La Robiline

Le Mont des Corvées, St Ouen

☎ 01534 482408

Open: Mar to end Oct 10am–5pm, daily. Admission charge. Large Car Park, Café. Disabled access.

Bouchet Agateware Pottery

Behind Parish Hall, St Ouen

☎ 01534 482345

www.agateware.co.uk

Open 7 days a week from 9am–5pm (phone for opening hours 15 Nov to 12 Feb). Disabled access.

Channel Islands Military Museum

Five Mile Road, St Ouen

Open: daily 10am–5pm, Easter to Oct.

Grève de Lecq Barracks

Grève de Lecq, St Mary

☎ 01534 483193

Information centre in Block 1. Open May to Sept. Wed to Sat 10am–5pm, Sun 1–5pm. Free admission.

Grosnez Castle

Near Grosnez Point, St Ouen

Ruins date from fourteenth century. Public free to wander.

Jersey Pearl

Five Mile Road, St Ouen

☎ 01534 862137

www.jerseypearl.com

Open 10am–5.30pm in summer

10am–4.30pm in winter. Disabled access. Airport Shop ☎ 01534 490364, Queen St, St Helier Shop ☎ 01534 633160 and Gorey Pier Shop ☎ 01534 855197

Kempt Tower Interpretation Centre

Five Mile Road, St Ouen

☎ 01534 483651

Open: May to end Sep, daily 2 5pm. No disabled access.

La Mare Wine Estate

Near Devil's Hole, St Mary

☎ 01534 481178

www.lamarewineestate.com

Open: Visitor centre April to end Oct, daily 10am–5pm. Christmas shop open Nov & Dec. Jan to Mar by appointment only. Admission charge.

St Ouen's Manor

St Ouen

Home of the Seigneur of St Ouen. Grounds only open for charity functions.

Treasures of Earth

La Route de L'Etacq, St Ouen

☎ 01534 484811

www.treasureearth.com

Open: Daliy, 10.30am–5pm daily, April to Sept; Tue, Thurs, Sat, Sun 10am–4pm in March.

Admission charge for the Crystal Cave Exhibition. Reduced admission for senior citizens and students; children under 5 free.

6. St Brelade and St Peter

Around St Brelade

The parish of St Brelade covers the south-west tip of the island and extends along the coast from St Aubin's, just west of Beaumont, round Noirmont Point, into St Brelade's Bay itself, round Corbière and then to the north up along St Ouen's Bay, just past Le Braye slipway. With such an extensive coastline, it has many attractive beaches to choose from as well as cliff walks with splendid views.

It was once thought that St Brelade might have been the sixth-century saint so famous for his voyages, St Brendan. Nowadays, though, the name St Brelade is thought to be a softened version of the Celtic name Bren Gwaladr or Branwallader. Branwallader was a Celtic monk and companion of the more famous St Sampson, who was supposed to have visited Jersey in the sixth-century. St Brendan's personal symbol – a silver fish on a blue background – is (now mistakenly) the parish emblem, as can be seen on the wall of the Parish Hall (*La Salle Paroissiale*) in St Aubin by the harbour.

Prehistoric Remains

For those interested in Jersey's prehistory, the most important site in the parish, as well as in the whole of Jersey, is at the east end of St Brelade's Bay at La Cotte Point. It is a cave, **La Cotte de St Brelade,** now some 60ft (18m) above sea level, first used in about 110,000BC, where not only food remains and flake tools have been found, but also mammoth and woolly rhinoceros bones. It is thought that the ravines in this cliff were used as 'gump traps' to catch these huge animals, as they were forced along the narrow strip of land to the drop below. This camping place is not accessible to the general public. Many of the items found in the cave are on display in the Jersey Museum in St Helier, as are the pots and implements from a Neolithic settlement excavated at Les Blanches Banques, further to the west of the parish.

Also from the Neolithic age are the heaps of fallen stones on the cliffs overlooking Fiquet Bay which were once two dolmens, while near **La Sergenté** off Le Mont de la Pulente are the remains of a round hut tomb, the earliest dolmen in Jersey. Several menhirs, or standing stones, among the grass-covered sand dunes of Les Quennevais, the **Blanches Banques Menhirs,** also bear witness to the pagan religious observances of those prehistoric times.

In and Around St Aubin

Whether prehistoric man ever had time to marvel at the many different bays and caves in St Brelade, today's visitors certainly can. Starting at the sheltered east corner of St Aubin's Bay there is the stretch of sand from the Gunsite slipway to St Aubin which is perfect for basking on and quite safe for bathing. Swimmers should take care, however, to avoid the area round **La Haule slipway** (*Bus 9, 12, 12a, 15*) which is reserved for waterskiers from the Jersey Sea Sport Centre.

After two or three lessons even a complete beginner should be able to enjoy the thrills and exhilaration of this increasingly popular water sport. Particularly popular with the young is wakeboarding, which is like snowboarding on water. Available for hire are jet-skis, which are 40 mph seascooters. The Jersey Sea Sport Centre is a Royal Yachting Association recognised teaching establishment. Also on La Haule Slip is Crusoe's Cabin, where breakfasts, lunches, light meals and teas are served. Also available for hire are surf jet and wet jet personal water craft. Surf jets are 30mph jet-powered surfboards (the easiest water sport), while wet jets are sea scooters.

Almost opposite St Helier harbour, is **St Aubin** (*Bus 12, 12a, 15*). There is a delightful promenade walk of about 3 miles (4.75km) between St Helier and here, as well as an easy cycle ride along the specially made track. As it is flat all the way, with a wonderful sea view, it also makes a popular course for joggers. In the summer there are waterskiers and other water sporting activities to watch; from November to spring, over-wintering brent geese, oystercatchers, redshanks and dunlin can be seen wading along the shore. The bright lights along the whole length of the prom make a colourful display on summer evenings.

On Le Boulevard, you will find **The Harbour Gallery**, open seven days a week; on display are works by local artists.

The best way for a visitor to enjoy St Aubin is to stroll round it. There is parking on the front to the east of the village from where it is only a step or two to the boatyard and harbour. Facing the harbour is La Salle Paroissiale de St Brelade (**St Brelade's Parish Hall**), which was once the Terminus Hotel and railway station of the Jersey Railway. This ran originally from St Helier to St Aubin and was then extended to Corbière. In 1936 the railway station was gutted by fire and the major part of the line's rolling stock was destroyed. Mystery surrounds the fire to this day. Whatever the cause, the important result was that the company decided to close

the railway, and so the bus took over as the island's sole form of public transport from that year.

Continuing along the Bulwarks, formerly known as Le Boulevard, with the harbour to the left, there are several fine houses lying back from the road which are worth looking at in passing. The **Old Court House** at the very end of the road is particularly interesting, as it was probably here that seventeenth-century privateers brought their booty for auction. Watchers of the television series, *Bergerac*, may also recognise it as 'The Royal Barge' where Diamante Lil used to be the hostess. Locals and visitors enjoy the view from its courtyard over the harbour and the bay beyond.

Over the road on the headland is the Royal Channel Islands Yacht Club, where visiting yachtsmen are always welcome.

The next road of architectural interest in St Aubin is the High Street, to the right up Mont les Vaux. The earliest houses, dating from around 1657, are at the bottom of the hill. Those at the top of the High Street were built in the nineteenth century. Many of the old granite cottages have 'marriage stones' with the initials of the husband and wife who owned them. The date on the stone could either be that of the marriage or when the house was built. The Sail Loft is a reminder of those days when shipbuilding was an important industry in St Aubin, before the advent of steam-powered boats.

Continuing up Mont les Vaux there are still two more places to see. On the right-hand side of the hill there is **St Aubin's church** itself, a pleasing example of Victorian Gothic. Inside there is the only pre-Raphaelite stained glass in Jersey – a fine window in the Lady Chapel by Edward Burne-Jones and William Morris.

On the bend further up the hill is a garden which intrigues everyone who passes it. The **Shell Garden** and all the ornaments in it are decorated throughout with the pearlescent shells of the ormer which used to be found so abundantly in Jersey waters. An unusual shot for the holiday album!

In St Aubin, there is a small group of shops, including a bank, a post office and a supermarket. There are also several restaurants, cafés and inns. All in all, a most attractive part of St Brelade's parish.

Bays, Beaches and Clifftops

Belcroute Bay

The next bay round the coast worth a visit is Belcroute (*Bus 12 or 12a and walk*). This can be reached by going along La Route de Noirmont and then, just before Portelet, bearing to the left down a steep narrow road, past the magnificent wrought iron gates of the privately owned Noirmont Manor. From this quiet, east-facing and sheltered bay, with its wooded backdrop, inhabited by tits, fly-catchers and goldcrests, the visitor can look right across St Aubin's Bay to Fort Regent.

Noirmont Point

Between the bays of Belcroute and Portelet comes the majestic headland of Noirmont (*Bus 12 or 12a and walk*), the Black Mount, of which Jerseymen say that when clouds gather over it, or '*quand Nôirmont met son bonnet*' (when Noirmont puts on its bonnet) it is sure to rain. There is so much of interest here: a wood with holm oaks to wander through and cliff paths to walk along; at the headland's point a German Occupation command bunker, complete with its K18 coastal artillery gun; at its foot Noirmont Tower, built between 1810 and 1814 against a French invasion

---

The Corbière (Railway) Walk

For the keen walker there is a flower and shrub-lined walk, The Corbière Walk, which follows the track where the railway used to run the 4 miles (6.5Km) from St Aubin up to Corbière. The number 12 bus goes frequently from Corbière back to St Aubin for those without the energy to walk back. The great block of red granite which lies opposite where the Corbière railway ticket office was is known as the **Table des Marthes**, as children used to play knucklebones (*marthes*) on it. Originally it was no doubt the capstone of a prehistoric tomb.

St Aubin's Harbour.

and now used as a lighthouse. In spring, nature lovers can spy the young herring gull and shag in their nests on the cliff ledges; inland the nests of the Dartford warbler; and all summer enjoy the sight and smell of its gorse and heather-covered slopes. On the grass-covered cliff slopes the rare autumn squill with its blue/white bells can be seen from July to September and, at its best on a sunny morning, the yellow spotted rock rose can be found. By the small pond to the south-west of the headland grows the unique, but sadly fast-declining, Jersey forget-me-not. Most importantly there is plenty of space for parking. The whole headland is kept by the States of Jersey as a war memorial to those who perished in World War II.

Portelet Bay

Returning from Noirmont Point towards La Route de Noirmont, there are two beaches and two commons to choose from. The first turning to the left leads down Portelet Lane to Portelet Bay (*Bus 12, 12a*). This is approached from the road by steep steps – not for the unfit – leading down to the beach which is surrounded on three sides by tree-covered cliffs. The sandy beach is small but charming and, despite the steep climb down, popular, because of its south-facing sheltered aspect.

A tragic tale is associated with the tiny **Ile au Guerdain** which lies in the centre of this small bay. A certain Philip Janvrin, born in the parish of St Brelade, sailed to Nantes in his ship the *Esther* but, when he came back in 1721 and wanted to anchor in St Aubin, he was refused permission to do so for fear of infection from the bubonic plague, then raging in that part of France. Instead his ship and its crew had to remain in quarantine in Belcroute Bay. Unfortunately, Philip Janvrin had indeed been infected by the plague and it was not long before he died of it, still aboard his ship.

The authorities continued to be adamant that even his dead body could not be brought ashore. Then, after intercession from his widow, a compromise was reached. Permission was given for him to be buried on the Ile au Guerdain, in sight of his St Brelade home. So, today, the island is known locally as 'Janvrin's Tomb', though Portelet Tower, built over the grave a hundred years later, is part of Jersey's defence against the French and not part of the memorial to poor Janvrin. He was later buried in St Brelade's cemetery. It should be noted that swimming in the waters round Janvrin's Tomb can be dangerous.

The second turning, down Portelet Road, leads to **Portelet Common**, an ideal spot for family picnics and rambles. The third turning to the left is the narrow Mont de Ouaisné (pronounced 'waynay') which leads down to the sandy beach of Ouaisné and the common. They can also both be reached by climbing down the cliff slope from Portelet Common by La Cotte Point, where the Palaeolithic cave is.

At **Ouaisné** (*Bus 12*), large gatherings of the great crested grebe have been seen in the spring, taking advantage of the bay's shelter. In the summer this south-west-facing beach is a favourite spot with families, as there is a large car park. Then as well as the fine stretch of sand there is the common behind the beach for picnics or exploring. The toilets have easy access for wheelchairs.

St Brelade's Bay

After the small, unspoilt bays of Belcroute and Portelet, the sweep of St Brelade's Bay (*Bus 12*) next to Ouaisné is quite a contrast, but it is also one of the most photogenic bays in the island, with its palm trees, colourfully laid-out gardens and extensive stretch of sand. St Brelade's beach can be reached from Ouaisné either by walking along the beach at low tide, or over the common which borders the beach. The approach to St Brelade's Bay by road is along the B57 from Noirmont and then down

Portelet Bay.

Mont Sohier (B66). There is plenty of space for parking in the car parks on the right-hand side of the road. The number 12 bus gives a frequent service from the Weighbridge to St Brelade's Bay.

St Brelade's parish church (*Bus 12*), dedicated to St Brelade, is at the west end of St Brelade's Bay. Built of local La Moye granite, with the sea coming up to the churchyard, it is probably the most picturesque church on the island. It dates from as early as the eleventh-century and the south, east and west walls of the original Norman building are still standing. Since then, however, numerous changes and additions have been made, including, at the end of the nineteenth-century, church pews in the then contemporary art nouveau style, which are still in use.

Two memorials distinguish the churchyard. The first is the obelisk given by the States of Jersey to commemorate the generous founder of the General Hospital, Mrs Marie Bartlet, who lived in the parish in the eighteenth-century. The second belongs to the twentieth-century and was given by Lady Trent in memory of her husband, Jesse Boot, the famous chemist, the first Lord Trent. The attractive lychgate makes a popular backdrop for the photographing of those married in the church.

Outside the church is a short footpath leading from the south door, down some granite steps, to the sea. This is the *perquage* or sanctuary path, which every island church had in the Middle Ages. It offered to those members of the parish who had broken the law a way of escape from the harsh torture and imprisonment that would await them if they were found guilty at their trial.

Many criminals chose to go down the *perquage* path to perpetual banishment from Jersey rather than face the rigours of the medieval penal system.

Right alongside the parish church is what is known as the **Fisherman's Chapel** (*Bus 12*), which may, in fact, mark the site of the original church. It, too, is built of local granite and dates back to the twelfth-century, when it seems to have been used as a mortuary chapel and then as a chantry chapel, where mass was said for the family who owned it. Its historical importance stems from the fact that it has the finest medieval wall paintings in the Channel Islands, which people from all over Europe come to see.

It was during the fourteenth and fifteenth centuries that the south and north walls of the chapel were painted with biblical scenes from the Old and New Testaments, including the Fall, Cain and Abel, the Annunciation, Palm Sunday and the Crucifixion. Over the altar is painted God the Father, appearing in the heavens and, below, the Virgin Mary with the sons of the owner's family kneeling on her left, and the daughters kneeling on the right. On the west wall, opposite the altar, is a depiction of the Last Judgement, reminiscent of the style of Stanley Spencer, with the medieval parishioners, complete with hats of the period, rising from their tombs to be judged by the figure of Christ.

This chapel may at one time have served as a place of worship for a guild of fishermen, but after the Reformation it was no longer used at all for religious purposes. In fact, for 300 years it was totally neglected, finally being used as a workshop. Only in 1933 was it restored as a place of worship, when an old altar slab with five consecration crosses, commemorating the five wounds of Christ on the cross, was brought from Mont Orgueil, and erected as the altar.

A history of both the church and the chapel can be found just inside the west door of the church, while an illustrated summary of the restoration of the wall paintings inside the Fisherman's Chapel can be seen on the outside of the north wall of the chapel itself.

Lining the front of St Brelade's Bay are hotels, restaurants and cafés; **Zanzina Art Gallery & Coffee Bar** and **Zanzibar Restaurant** overlook the bay and on the beach there are deckchairs and windbreaks for hire.

There is also a **Windsurfing and Sailing School** at the Wayside slip in St Brelade's Bay. Here beginners can enjoy tranquil sea conditions in Mediterranean-style surroundings. There are canoes, sailing dinghies and windsurfer equipment to hire as well as instruction in sailing and windsurfing.

St Brelade's Bay is an extremely popular beach, perfect with its sheltered position for both sunbathing and safe swimming at all stages of the tide as well as watersports. During the summer the beach is patrolled by beach guards. It also looks most picturesque from the sea during one of the boat trips that can be taken round the bay. For anyone who wants a change from sea and sand, there is the **Winston Churchill Memorial Park** on the other side of the coast road, with its climbing roses, miniature waterfall and seats in the sun or shade.

From the far west end of St Brelade's Bay there is easy access to an ideal and quiet picnic spot. Follow the white railings by the jetty up to a signpost which reads Le Coléron and walk up the narrow path by the side of it and out onto the headland. Here there is a seat surrounded by gorse, broom and other wild flowers from which St Brelade's Bay can be viewed to the left and Bouilly Port (above which is the resting place of the famous chemist Jesse Boot) lies overlooking the bay, to the right.

Beauport

This south-west corner of the island has three more beaches which are worth a visit; the next round the coast is Beauport (*Bus 12*). From the footpath between St Brelade's church and the cemetery a little way along it, there is a well-signposted 20-minute walk over the cliffs to Beauport, or it can be reached by car from either end of Mont ès Croix. The eastern end goes past St Brelade's church hall, opposite the church, and the western end is reached from Route Orange. Both approaches are clearly signposted. There is a car park but no toilet facilities above Beauport and the beach is reached by going down a path which winds for about 5 minutes' walk through the bracken to the golden sands below. This bay, with its sparkling sea, has been kept unspoiled and is well loved for its seclusion and good swimming by locals and visitors alike. It should be noted that no refreshment facilities are available either on the beach or on the cliffs above it.

Corbière

Before coming to the next small beach along the parish's Atlantic coast, St Brelade offers the visitor the lonely

153

The Fisherman's Chapel with its medieval wall paintings, St Brelades Bay.

Beauport Bay.

splendour of the **Corbière lighthouse** (*Bus 12*) on its extreme south-western tip. Its name comes from *corbeau*, the French for a crow, rook or raven, once considered birds of ill omen, and, therefore, appropriate for dangerous rocks that brought many a ship to disaster and many a sailor to a watery grave. Yet a lighthouse was not built to warn of their danger until 1873. The States chose Imrie Bell to construct it and he built a 35ft (10.5m)-high concrete tower on a 9ft (2.7m)-high concrete platform – the first concrete lighthouse in the British Isles. The beam from its powerful, automatic light can be seen over a distance of nearly 20 miles.

The rocks are still a hazard to those on foot, however, because although there is a natural causeway to the lighthouse at low tide, when the tide turns the seas cover the path at an incredible speed. There is a memorial stone at Corbière which acts as a constant reminder of the dangerous rush of the tide and reads 'Peter Edwin Larbalestier, assistant keeper at the lighthouse, who on the 28th of May, 1946 gave his life in attempting to rescue a visitor cut off by the incoming tide. Take heed, all ye that pass by!'

The second tower on the headland was an observation tower built by the Germans, with the help of their slave labour force, during the Occupation.

It is now used by Jersey Radio as a marine coast station. The headland can be reached by car along La Rue de la Corbière, by the number 12 bus, or on foot up The Corbière Walk from St Aubin, which is even pleasanter to walk down. The tower south of La Rue de la Corbière is part of the sea water desalination plant which ensures a constant water supply for islanders, even in time of drought.

The Atlantic-Facing Coast

The last two beaches to visit in the parish face due west. First comes **Petit Port** (*Bus 12*), just round the road from Corbière, which can be reached on the B44 Corbière to Petit Port road which comes sweeping down past gorse-covered hills to the no-through-road on the left, where there is the car park for the beach. When the tide is out, this is more a beach for sunbathing on, or rock clambering, rather than swimming, as the receding tide leaves only small rock pools behind.

Petit Port is a good starting point, though, for a short cliff walk around the headland to St Ouen's Bay, the largest bay in the island. The walk starts either past four concrete posts at the entrance to the car park or by the sea wall. If the latter

Corbière Lighthouse.

is taken, there are extensive German fortifications to the left of the path and then the sweep of St Ouen's Bay from L'Oeillère (the 'Look Out') along the 5 sandy miles (8km) to Etacquerel, with La Rocco Tower in the foreground and, on a clear day, Sark and Guernsey on the distant horizon. This footpath is lined here and there with the fragantly scented white-flowered burnet roses and leads to La Pulente in about 20 minutes.

La Pulente is an ideal beach for the active visitor as well as the sunbather, because of its extent both across and down to the sea. Once famed for its seaweed or vraic gatherers, and still plentifully covered with small shells, La Pulente is now a favourite spot for all-year-round jogging, which can continue right round the bay. To the north at Le Braye slip (*Bus 12a*) sand car and motor cycle races are held, while further along the beach the Atlantic rollers make this the best spot on the island for surfing. There is parking, as well as toilets and refreshments, at both La Pulente and Le Braye. Nature lovers may like to note that to the north, at Le Braye slip, (*Bus 12a*), behind the sea wall, grows the saltmarsh species of sea purslane together with the South African 'mesem' Disphyma, which are obviously not to be picked.

The dunes behind these west-facing beaches belong to one of the most extensive dune systems in the British Isles. Springing through the coarse turf is an abundance of wild flowers; some so small that one has to kneel down to spot them. Here grow different kinds of orchid, including the early purple, the green winged and the pyramidal, as well as hare's tail grass, Atlantic clover and the sand crocus.

Les Quennevais Shopping Centre

(*Bus 12, 12a, 15*)

It would be a mistake to think that St Brelade offers only seaside pleasures. On the contrary, it offers at Les Quennevais the largest shopping complex outside St Helier. The name Quennevais comes from *chèrevière* or *chanevière*, meaning a place where hemp is grown, for this was an important crop when ropes made of hemp were needed for the island's shipbuilding industry.

To return to the shopping facilities at Les Quennevais, there are, in fact, three distinct centres, all developed in the 1950s or 60s. Driving south from the airport, along L'Avenue de la Commune and then La Route des Quennevais, the first shops on the left, built round three sides of the car park with a large supermarket in the centre, are known as Les Quennevais Parade. Tucked just behind the Parade, on the right, is Les Quennevais Precinct, whose shops have the advantage of a large car park at the back.

There is an attraction here for children called the **Elephant Park**, right opposite the Country Park, where there is plenty of space for free parking. It can be reached either by the Corbières Walk, when it reaches Les Quennevais Precinct, or by walking east behind the Precinct's shops. At this children's playground there are two climbing frames, one specially for toddlers; a small helter skelter ride; an elephant slide; 2 see-saws; swings for babies as well as for older children; a balancing beam and bouncing animals, as well as a sandpit.

Then, on the four corners of the

crossroads where Route Orange meets La Rue Don is the third shopping and parking area (complete with toilet facilities), known as Red Houses. Together these three centres will provide for almost every shopper's needs from banking to DIY, including clothes, food, hairdressing, chemists, travel agents, record centres, cleaners, cafés and restaurants – even dentists and doctors. So comprehensive is the range of goods and services on offer and so convenient the parking at Les Quennevais, many islanders do their shopping here in preference to the busier St Helier.

Places to Visit

As well as opportunities to delve into the past, sample coves and beaches, and to shop, St Brelade still has more to tempt the visitor.

The entrance to **Pont Marquet Country Park** (*Bus 15*) is on the right down La Petite Route des Mielles travelling north and it has its own car park. A ramble round the park with its fine pines and chestnut trees could take anything from half an hour to an hour or the ramble could be extended by walking some distance along The Corbière Walk from St Aubin to Corbière, which lies by the side of the park. It is also an ideal spot for a picnic, with its wild flowers and tranquil atmosphere.

For children who might be too young to enjoy the unspoilt pleasures of the park, on the other side of La Petite Route des Mielles there is a playground. This has a sandpit, climbing frame, swings, see saw and chute for the youngsters to play on, with sheltered seats where parents can sit. There are also toilet facilities.

The **Jersey Lavender Farm** is on La Rue du Pont Marquet, 5 minutes walk from the bus stops at Silver Springs Hotel and Red Houses, which are served by the 12, 12a and 15 buses. The most interesting time to visit is when the lavender is harvested in July and August. Then visitors can see the cutting and gathering of the crop from the fields, watch the steam distillation of the lavender oil and go through the room where the perfume is bottled. A full range of the Jersey Lavender products, including potted lavender plants, are on sale in the Lavender Shop.

But even when it is not harvest time there is still plenty to do and see. For the energetic there are the three main lavender fields to walk round, with benches for those who want to enjoy the view. In the main garden, as well as several sculptures, there are also over 50 different types of bamboos to see. There is also a genuine gypsy caravan, over 150 years old, as well as a herb garden and a dovecote, not forgetting the beehives from which comes the predominantly lavender honey on sale in the shop. There is a restaurant with a verandah from which to view the fragrant fields.

For those with specialised interests, there are facilities in the parish to enjoy indoor and outdoor sport. The **Les Quennevais Sports Centre** is at Don Farm, Les Quennevais. It provides facilities outside for hockey, rugby, cricket, football and tennis, pétanque and athletics There are also a 1,640yd (1,500m) road cycle track and bowling greens. In the indoor sports hall badminton, squash, table tennis, volleyball and basketball can be played.

157

Lavender Farm.

A building housing two indoor swimming pools is at the Sports Centre. The main pool is 27yds (25 metres) long and has eight lanes, making it ideal for training. There is a second smaller pool with disabled access which is 20yds (18 metres) by 13yds (12 metres), and a separate sauna and steam room. On the first floor above the pools there is the 'Sports-view' bar and restaurant, looking out over the pools and the multi-purpose sports hall. Tennis courts and squash courts can be hired. All sports equipment is available for hire.

All these sporting activities are available to visitors. Also throughout the season the keenly contested Summer League football matches between local hotel sides are played here, which visitors might enjoy watching.

La Moye

There is an 18-hole golf course at La Moye, off La Route Orange, but visitors must be members of a recognised golf club. It is at **La Moye Golf Club** (*Bus 12 and 12a to both golf and music club*) that the European Senior Classic Golf Tournament is held, usually in June.

During the summer **Nashville Country Music Club** meet every Wednesday at La Moye Ballroom and Bars on La Route Orange. Meetings,

Above: Living Legend

Left: Catherine Best jewellery studio and Windmill Restaurant.

Below: Le Moulin de Quetivel.

at which both local and visiting groups perform and for which there is an admission charge, start at 8.45pm and continue till midnight.

Those interested in croquet might like to have a game with members of the Jersey Croquet Club at Les Quennevais Sports Centre.

St Peter

St Peter may only have a couple of short coastlines – in the bays of St Aubin in the south and St Ouen in the west, but what a host of other attractions this parish has to offer inland. There is the natural beauty of St Peter's Valley and its various tourist spots. Then there is the heart of the parish, with several different places to visit, centred round the church. Perhaps, even more importantly for the island's visitors, it is the parish where Jersey's airport is sited.

St Peter's Valley

St Peter's Valley (*Bus 8,*) is one of the five picturesque valleys that cut across the island from north to south and for many centuries it was considered the most beautiful of them all. In fact, when Queen Victoria asked to see the loveliest view in Jersey on her visit here in 1858, she was taken for a drive through St Peter's Valley.

It still has its rural charm, especially in the early months of the year: its hillsides dotted with lent lilies and other wild flowers; the tall iris marking the course of the stream, with its splash of yellow; the distinctive catkins of the sweet chestnut yellow in the woodland; the red squirrels sometimes glimpsed round the fine oaks searching for hidden acorns.

Regrettably, though, the German Occupation left more than one ugly mark on the valley. For here, in the centre of the island, the occupying forces built not only their Underground Hospital in St Lawrence, but also a power station, a pumping station and three huge ammunition tunnels. Some of the thousands of tons of rocks and rubble removed in these excavations were used, 7 years after Jersey had been liberated, in the construction of the runway at the airport. What was left in the valley is now almost completely grown over with natural vegetation and is no longer the eyesore that once it was.

Nearly at the southernmost tip of St Peter's Valley, on the B58 Mont Fallu, is a second attraction. This is **Le Moulin de Quetivel**, a National Trust property, which was mentioned as one of the island's thirty-eight watermills as early as 1309. It was also one of the eight mills which, at one time or another, were served by St Peter's Valley stream which still powers it.

The mill was worked from the fourteenth-century right down to the nineteenth-century, but then fell into disrepair. By 1934 only the iron rims of the watermill remained in the way of machinery and the building itself was badly in need of repair. But, during the German Occupation, Le Moulin de Quetivel had a reprieve – the Germans ordered local craftsmen to repair it so that once again it could grind grain.

After the end of the war, the mill was of no further use until, in 1979, it was decided that it should be restored and become fully operational again. It would grind locally grown corn that would then be sold as stoneground flour. Today visitors can see how Le Moulin de Quetivel works and buy what it produces. There is also a display on the top floor showing the milling process through the ages and charting the history of the mills in Jersey. The shop on the ground floor sells the flour, together with locally made preserves and craft items such as prints and cards. A helpful leaflet which is available on admission, explains what happens on each floor. The ladder steps up to the different floors of the mill are steep, though, and would not be suitable for anyone who is disabled.

The pastoral setting of Le Moulin de Quetivel, however, should not be missed, with its yellow irises in spring and many wild flowers colouring the meadows in the summer. The mill can also be reached by a rustic path. This starts by the car park almost directly opposite the Victoria inn and goes through the woods until it comes to the second of the mill's car parks, opposite Sorrel Stables and Saddlery. This is a short peaceful walk, past the mill pond with its ducks and other water fowl, through the trees, several with nesting boxes on them and where sometimes a red squirrel can be glimpsed, and down some steps to the mill itself. This walk now extends down to Le Moulin de Tesson, the lowest of St Peter's watermills, which is also owned by the National Trust of Jersey and is currently undergoing restoration

There is also an authentically restored windmill in the parish, which is now home to the **Catherine Best** jewellery studio. Catherine Best has received worldwide recognition for her innovative creations. Individual commissions can normally be produced within 24 hours. The 120 seater **Windmill Restaurant** is open daily for lunch and dinner.

The Windmill is located off the B53 on Les Chenolles, going west after St Mary's parish church.

For horse riders there are stables in St Peter's Valley. **Sorrel Stables and Saddlery Centre** (*Bus 8*), at the bottom of Le Mont Fallu as it comes into St Peter's Valley, have their own two large outdoor sand schools. In one sanded field ½-hour lunge lessons (a long rope is attached to the horse) can be given by experienced staff to young children and beginners; in another there are jumping and cross-country facilities for experienced riders. Riding gear, such as hat and wellies, can be hired at no extra charge. Visitors are welcome to come and look at the horses and will also find a complete range of equestrian equipment for sale, as well as gifts with horse lovers in mind. What better way to discover the rural beauties of this western parish than from the saddle!

Situated at the far north end of St Peters is **Living Legend**. It has three main parts – The Jersey Experience, Adventure Golf and a Go-Karting track. The Jersey Experience is an award winning special effects show with a film featuring various well known actors such as John Nettles and Kevin Whately plus actress Samantha Janus. Explore local myths, legends and history on a unique voyage of discovery. The three-acre mini-golf course is set amid a beautiful garden with various skill levels for you to choose from. If your kids are up to it, try the Formula One style karting track. If you have been karting previously, you are promised much more! This attraction also has a range of shopping and eating options. It is situated at La Rue du Petit Aleval, off St Peter's Valley.

St Peter's Village

The second centre to visit in St Peter's parish is the village (*Bus 9*), which clusters round the church. Here there is the Parish Hall, with its typical Jersey architecture, the Youth and Community Centre, a large park, a supermarket, a food hall and a post office.

The chapel from which **St Peter's church** originated is now the chancel which, in common with others on the island, is older than the rest of the church. The chancel walls, which are nearly 4ft (1.2m) thick and built of stones from the beach, probably date back to before 1066. The major enlargements came in the twelfth-century – when the building took the shape of a cross with the additional nave and transepts – in the fourteenth and fifteenth-centuries and, finally, in the nineteenth-century, when the north aisle was added.

Its spire of 120ft (36.5m) is the tallest in Jersey and has been struck by lightning three times since it was added to the church tower in the fifteenth-century. Today, unique among church steeples, it carries at its tip a red warning light for planes using the nearby airport.

Notable features inside the church are a triptych featuring the Virgin Mary, the altar in the arched niche of the Lady Chapel and a finely carved altarpiece depicting the Last Supper.

For visitors who are staying in one of the hotels or guest houses near St Peter it is good to know that the Youth and Community Centre welcomes holidaymakers. The youth club and senior citizens club meet weekly. Tea rooms are open daily 8am–4.40pm.

Around the Parish

This parish, which has St Peter's keys of heaven for its emblem, does not only have relics of World War II; there is a cannon at Beaumont crossroads, on the way up to the airport from the south coast, which is over 400 years old. It was originally built in Houndsditch and is one of only two of the same kind still in existence. On it are the words: 'JHON [*sic*] OWEN MADE THIS PESE ANNO DNI 1551 FOR THE PARYSHE OF SAYNT PETER IN JERSSE.'

St Peter also has the unhappy distinction of being the parish where, during the English Civil War, Cromwell's forces successfully invaded the island and kept it under Parliamentarian rule for 9 years. It happened in 1651, on 22 October, when Cromwell's Admiral Blake, with a fleet of eighty ships, sailed up and down – some say waiting for the heavy surf to subside – the whole length of St Ouen's Bay for 2 whole days. Ready to repulse any landing, the Royalist Jersey Army marched up and down the coast between L'Etacq and St Brelade to keep a wary eye for an enemy attack. So by the time the Parliamentarian forces eventually landed on the beach in the middle of the night, de Carteret and his Jersey soldiers were quite worn out. Though the island's defenders put up a desperate fight, they finally had to retreat to Elizabeth Castle. By December that year, St Aubin's Fort, Mont Orgueil Castle and Elizabeth Castle were all forced to surrender and the commander of the English invasion forces, the Roundhead Colonel Heane, was made Governor of Jersey.

Sunset Nurseries Flower Centre (*Bus 12a*) is a mile (1.6km) inland from St Ouen's Bay at the top of the lane from the Western Golf Range. On sale in this flower centre are not only Jersey lily bulbs, seeds and dried flowers, but also an extensive range of quality gifts including leatherware, soft toys and costume jewellery. From here it is also possible to send carnations or freesias by post to any address in the UK, or Europe, or even have a box made up to carry home.

Visitors can enter the glasshouses where carnations and Peruvian lilies grow; look into the tropical bird garden; have a coffee, lunch, tea, even an all-day breakfast, in the flower-festooned and covered tea-garden; and enjoy the miniature tropical garden, where there is the constant sound of running water.

The main operation of the nurseries is the production of cut flowers and the most important crop are the Peruvian Lilies. Their rhyzomes are planted straight into the soil and picking begins after 4 or 5 months. An automatic irrigation system gives the plants all the water and fertiliser they need. The correct temperature is kept constant by automatic heating and ventilation, and so flowers are produced all the year round.

There is one activity in St Peter which takes full advantage of the terrain of sand dunes on the western coast – golf. The **Les Mielles Golf Course** (*Bus 12a*) is to be found in the centre of St Ouen's Bay, where the Five Mile Road makes the corner with La Route de la Marette. Visitors are welcome and here there is an 18-hole golf course and activity centre consisting of a driving range, miniature

golf and laser clay pigeon shooting. On site Rocco's restaurant and bar is open daily with seasonal barbecues.

The spectator sport to watch in this parish, however, is rugby. All important games are played at the **Jersey Rugby Club** (*Bus 9*), on the left of the B36 on the way up to the airport from St Helier. Details of forthcoming matches can be obtained by calling Tourism; by looking at the sports pages of the *Jersey Evening Post* or by listening to BBC Radio Jersey between 7am and 9am. At Easter the Hockey Festival, also involving teams from away, is played here too.

Another sporting attraction in this parish is the **Jersey Bowl** ten-pin bowling alley, near the rugby club, on the main road going towards the airport from St Peter and St Helier. There are 18 lanes open daily 12am–12pm. Other attractions on site include Quasar, a pool hall and an indoor play area for the younger children. There is also a bar, restaurant, southern fried chicken and al fresco barbecue.

For the majority of visitors, St Peter is the first parish they set foot in because it was here, in 1937, that the States built the island's **airport** (*Bus 15 every 15 minutes*). But Jersey's aviation history goes, incredibly, right back to 1790, when a hot air balloon was launched from the hospital grounds and flew over the island. Islanders had to wait over 120 years, though, before they saw a real aircraft in Jersey. That happened in 1912, when one of the competitors in the St Malo–Jersey–St Malo Race landed his Sanchez-Beza biplane mid-route in St Aubin's Bay before – appreciably delayed by inquisitive islanders who had never seen a plane before – continuing on his way. Seven years later, today's routine of flying the UK newspapers daily into the island had a forerunner, when *Lloyds Weekly News* was flown in during a rail strike in England.

It was the 1920s and 1930s which saw the start and great acceleration of passenger air traffic to the island. The landing strip was the beach in St Aubin's Bay; the aircraft were seaplanes, de Havillands, Dragons and Rapides and the destinations Portsmouth, Southampton and London; the price of a return ticket from St Helier to Victoria Station – a 3-hour journey – was £5, quite a sum between the wars. In 1936 alone, 30,000 passengers were flown in and out of the island.

Plans for an inland airport – the disadvantage of landing on the beach was that it could only be done at low tide – had begun as early as 1930, but it was not until 1937 that the 218 vergée site, earmarked by the States in St Peter, had been transformed into an airport, with four grassed flightways, at a cost of £128,000.

Only 3 years after the Bailiff's wife had opened the airport, Britain and Germany were at war. Then passenger services were severely restricted, and, for a time, the airport was used by a squadron of the Fleet Air Arm for training purposes. Later on, it was used by the RAF for a nightstop and refuelling base on bombing raids in Germany and Italy.

Once Churchill had declared, after the fall of France in June 1940, that the Channel Islands were demilitarised and would not be defended by British troops in the event of a German invasion, the airport had yet another new role to play.

It mobilised its ten and twelve-seater aircraft to evacuate, in just 2 days, over 300 islanders who wanted to spend the rest of the war in the UK.

Then came the final blow for Jersey. At 11 o'clock on 1 July, a German plane approached the airport. When it landed, a German Air Force Officer told the airport officials – in perfect English – that he wanted to speak to the Bailiff, to make sure that he had received the Nazi ultimatum, demanding the surrender of Jersey to the Occupation force which would be arriving that same afternoon. So it was that the Bailiff, in the company of the Attorney General, met the first Germans on British soil at the airport.

Today, nearly two million passengers pass through the airport each year, and it receives commercial aircraft from some 80 UK and European towns and cities annually. A major £26m redevelopment of the passenger facilities has prepared the airport to meet the service levels expected by the twenty-first century traveller. Jersey's own meteorological station, whose regular weather forecasts can be heard on BBC Radio Jersey, is also part of the airport complex.

To complete this survey of St Peter where it began, with its coastline, there is good safe swimming on its sandy southern beach in **St Aubin's Bay** (*Bus 12, 12a, 15*) between Beaumont and the Gunsite slipway. St Peter's western coast is part of the magnificent sandy sweep of **St Ouen's Bay** (*Bus 12a*), shared by three parishes, where the Atlantic rollers break and where the surfers have their fun. There is a surfing school and hire facilities as well as windsurfing equipment at the Sands Surf and Sail Centre on La Grande Route des Mielles.

Places to Visit

Catherine Best Jewellery

The Windmill, Les Chenolles, St. Peter

☎ 01534 485777 (studio)

☎ 01534 486555

(The Windmill Restaurant).

www.catherinebest.com

Studio open: Mon–Sat 9am–5.30pm
Sundays 9.30–5pm.

Corbière Lighthouse

Corbière, St Brelade

Built 1873, first concrete lighthouse in
the British Isles. Public free to wander
outside only.

Harbour Gallery

Le Boulevard, St Aubin

☎ 01534 743044

Gallery and craft studios

Open: daily, 10.30am–5.30pm

Jersey Lavender Farm

Rue du Pont Marquet,
St Brelade

☎ 01534 742933

www.jerseylavender.co.uk

Open: April to Sep.

Tue to Sun 10am–5pm.
Admission charge.
Disabled access.

Le Moulin de Quetivel (N.T.)

St Peter's Valley, St Peter

☎ 01534 483193 (mornings only)
/01534 45408

Open: May to Sept, Sat only, 10am–
4pm .Admission charge for non-
members of Trust.

The Living Legend

La Rue du Petit Aleval, St Peter

☎ 01534 485496

www.jerseyslivinglegend.je

Audio-visual history of Jersey and
adventure golf courses. Admission
charge. Disabled access.

Open: Daily, 9.30am 5pm Apr to Oct,
Sat–Wed, 9.30am-5pm Mar and Nov.

Portelet Tower or
Janvrin's Tomb

Ile au Guerdain, Portelet Bay

Public free to wander.

St Aubin's Fort

On island in St Aubin's Bay

Public free to wander

Sunset Nurseries

St Ouen's Bay, St Peter

☎ 01534 482090

www.sunsetnurseries.com

Open: daily 10am–5pm in season.
Winter: Mon–Fri, 10am-4.30pm
only except Christmas & New Year.
Tropical gardens, aviary, souvenirs.

Youth and Community Centre

St Peter's Village, St Peter

☎ 01534 483011

Open 8.30am–1.30pm Mon–Fri.
Tearoom open 9am–4.30pm

Accommodation

The independent visitor will find a variety of accommodation and offers on the internet. For unbiased advice and reservations, contact Jersey Tourist Information. It is advisable to book in advance during the busy tourist season.

Jersey Tourist Information
Liberation Square
St Helier
☎ 01534 448877
www.jersey.com

Jersey Travel Service
☎ 0844 770 8082
www.jerseytravelservice.co.uk

Art Galleries

Falle Fine Art
18 Hill Street
St Helier
☎ 01534 887877
www.fallefineart.com
Offers a wide range of post-1900 pieces.

Grange Gallery & Fine Arts
10 Victoria Road
Georgetown
St Saviour
☎ 01534 720077
Works by 19th and 20th century artists.

The Harbour Gallery
Le Boulevard
St Aubin
☎ 01534 743044
Gallery and craft studios
Open: daily,10.30am–5.30pm

Jersey Arts Centre and Berni Gallery
Phillips Street
St Helier
☎ 01534 700400
Arts Centre Office

Open: 9.30am–5.30pm Mon–Fri.

Gallery open: 10am–10pm
Restaurant open: Mon–Sat 10am–2.30pm and 5.30
onwards; Lunch 12 noon–2pm and theatre dinners from 6.30pm

Sir Francis Cook Gallery
(Jersey Heritage Trust)
Route de la Trinité,
Augrès, Trinity
☎ 01534 863333
Open: during exhibitions only
Admission free. Disabled visitors welcome.

Studio 18
23A Beresford Street
St Helier
☎ 01534 734920
www.studio18.co.uk
Contemporary works by leading local and international artists.

Victoria Art Gallery
3 Victoria Street
St Helier
☎ 01534 730279
www.victoriaartgallery.co.uk
Stocks originals, limited edition prints, silk screens and etchings by local and
international artists.

Driving in Jersey

Car Hire
Rates, usually including insurance and petrol, are less expensive than on the
mainland. Cars delivered to and collected from hotels, harbour or airport at no
extra charge. Hirers must be over 20; a current driving licence (held for at least a
year and no endorsements for dangerous or drunken driving for the last 5 years)
must be produced when hiring.

Zebra Hire cars
9 Esplanade
St Helier
☎ 01534 736556
www.zebrahire.com

Avis
Le Cappellains Garage
St Peter
☎ 01534 519100/0800 735 1110
www.avisjersey.co.uk

Europcar
Airport desk, Arrivals Hall
Jersey Airport
☎ 0800 735 0735/01534 747770
www.europcarjersey.com

Hertz
Alares House, Jersey Airport
☎ 0800 735 1014
www.hertzci.com

Jersey Classic Car Hire
22 Rouge Bouillion,St Helier
☎ 01534 746273
www.jerseyclassiccarhire.com

Sovereign Hire Cars
27 Esplanade, St Helier
☎ 01534 608062
www.carhire-jersey.com

Viceroy Hire Cars
63 The Esplanade, St Helier
☎ 01534 738698

Highway Code

There are two major points from Jersey's highway code for visiting drivers to remember. The first is that the MAXIMUM SPEED LIMIT IS 40MPH. Lower speed limits apply on certain stretches of road in built-up areas. The second applies in the case of an accident. The duties of any driver involved in an accident are threefold:

1 To stop immediately.
2 To leave the vehicle where it has stopped, unless given police permission to remove it.
3 To notify the police or, in a country area, the nearest local Centenier, whose name can be found at the front of the telephone directory.

Riders of motor cycles or mopeds are required by law to wear a helmet. Anyone on the road coming across the sign 'Filter in Turn' should negotiate the junction in turn with other vehicles in joining or crossing any stream of traffic. A yellow line across the road at a junction is a stop sign; it indicates entry to a main road. Where there is a single yellow line parallel to the kerb or roadside, parking is prohibited AT ALL TIMES.

Parking

Pay Cards: used for payment for parking throughout Jersey, Monday to Saturday 8am–5pm (until10pm on Gorey Pier). You must use them whenever you park on-street in the RED and YELLOW zones and in all car parks where you see the distinctive sign. You can buy books of paycards from the car ferry or Tourist Information Office in St Helier and from 200 shops, garages and post offices throughout Jersey. You must have paycards with you when you park so be prepared. Scratching off the silver foil on the card indicates the date, day and time, informing car park officials of the time of arrival and duration of stay. Display the validated paycards face-up on the dashboard of your car.

'Blue Badge' Scheme: Some restrictions apply. Contact the Town Hall for leaflet giving details ☎ 01534 811811 or 445509.

Parking in St Helier

Multi-storey Car Parks: Green Street, Minden Place, Sand Street, Patriotic Street, Pier Road and La Route de Port Elizabeth (Waterfront).

Other Car Parks: The Parade, Weighbridge, Minden Place (rear of Forum cinema), La Route du Fort, Midvale Road, Elizabeth Lane, People's Park, Gas Place, Inn on the Park, nelson Street, and Esplanade.

Entertainments and shows

Cabarets
many hotels provide cabaret and dancing during the summer season. See the *Jersey Evening Post* for details.

Cinoma
Cineworld
Waterfront Centre, St Helier
☎ 0871 200 2000 (Booking & info).
www.clneworld.co.uk
10-screen cinema

Clubs & Bars
Havana Club
Halkett Street, St Helier
Three dancefloors; 60s, 70s and 80s music.
☎ 01534 873848

Liquid Nightclub
Waterfront, St Helier
1,000 capacity nightclub.
☎ 01534 789356

see www.jersey.com for more information on Jersey's nightlife.

Theatre & Concerts
Jersey Arts Centre
Phillips Street, St Helier
Box Office ☎ 01534 700444. Disabled access.
www.thisisjersey.co.uk/jac

Gloucester Hall and Piazza
Fort Regent, St Helier
☎ 01534 449600

Opera House
Gloucester Street
St Helier
☎ 01534 511115 (Box office)
www.jerseyoperahouse.co.uk
Box office open Monday to Saturday 10am-5.30pm, 8pm on show nights and one hour before shows on Sundays.

Fort Regent
Entertainment Centre
St Helier
☎ 01534 449600 (or 449827 for credit card bookings for concerts).
Gloucester Hall: Tickets for Piazza evening shows are available from the Booking Office, Main Reception, Fort Regent.
Live Music & Dancing.

Getting around the island

Bicycle Hire
Simple, inexpensive. Deposit usually required.

Funbikes
St Aubin's Bay Promenade
☎ 01534 746780
www.littletrain.co.uk
Four-wheeled 'fun bikes' as well as the standard two-wheeled variety

The Hire Shop
St Aubin's Road, Millbrook
☎ 01534 873699
Pushchairs and wheelchairs, bikes and mopeds for hire.

Zebra Cycles
9 Esplanade,
St Helier
☎ 01534 736556
www.zebrahire.com

Jersey Bike Repairs
☎ 07797 914452
www.jerseybikerepairs.com

Cycle Tours
Funky P's Bike Hire
La Mare Wine Estate
☎ 01534 878187
www.jerseybikehire.co.uk

Jersey Cycle Tours
St Aubin
☎ 01534 746780
Guided cycle tours

Pure Adventure
☎ 01534 769165
www.purejersey.com

Bus Service
Connex Transport buses operate from a central bus and coach station at the Weighbridge, St Helier; for enquiries (including visitors who require wheelchair access) ☎ 01534 877772 or www.mybus.je for further information. Visitors who wish to use this service are advised to buy a timetable from the Tourist Information Centre.

Island Explorer
☎ 01534 87772
www.mybus.je
This is an easy to use hop-on, hop-off coach service linking Jersey's bays and attractions. It operates from mid-April to mid-October. Explorer tickets cover all links and under 16s travel free.

Coach Tours
A number of coach companies operate morning, afternoon or full day tours. Also evening drives to shows, cabarets and pubs. Information from hotels, guesthouses or direct from the coach companies – telephone numbers in Yellow Pages, under Coach Tour Operators.

Les Petits Trains de Jersey
Routes and starting points vary. For current information contact the Tourist Information Desk, Liberation Square, St Helier ☎ 01534 448877.
   Lillie and *Terence* depart opposite the Grand Hotel and run around the bay to St Aubin every hour. *Major Peirson* departs from Liberation square every hour on an historical tour of St Helier. All trains operate on a seasonal basis between 10.30am and 5pm.

Tantivy Blue Coach Tours
☎ 01534 706706
www.tantivybluecoach.com
Luxury coach tours visiting Jersey's favourite attractions.

Motorcycle/Scooter/Moped Hire

Hirers must be 18+ with a valid driving licence for at least 6 months. Crash helmets compulsory. Helmets and third party insurance included in hire cost. Deposits required.

Motorama
18 Great Union Road, St Helier
☎ 01534 722819
http://motorama-jersey.co.uk/hire

Taxi Ranks & Cabs

Taxi ranks are to be found outside the arrivals building at the airport and at the following locations in St Helier: Broad Street, Snow Hill, Weighbridge.

A and R Airport Taxis
☎ 07797 716121

Arrow-Luxicabs
☎ 01534 887000

Citicabs
☎ 01534 499999

Clarendon Dragons
☎ 01534 871111

Domino Cabs
☎ 01534 747047

Hail a Cab
☎ 01534 629600

Island Cabs
☎ 01534 625625

Motorama
18 Great Union Road, St Helier
☎ 01534 722819
http://motorama-jersey.co.uk/hire

Yellow Cabs
☎ 01534 888888

Getting to and from Jersey

Access to Jersey itself from the British mainland is frequent and direct from most of the major airports during the summer months. Ferry services operate from Portsmouth, Weymouth and Poole. Condor Ferries (reservations) ☎ 0870 243

5100, 01534 872240, www.condorferries.co.uk. Details of charter flights, winter breaks, package holidays, hotels, guest houses, self-catering accommodation and camping facilities can be obtained from any UK travel agent or by applying direct to Jersey Tourism, Liberation Square, St Helier (☎ 01534 448877). It you can be flexible with your depature dates there are some very competitive prices to be found on the internet, especially with the ever increasing number of budget airlines now operating from the UK.

Channel Islands Travel Service

Heron House
Jersey Airport
St Peter
☎ 01534 496600
www.jerseytravel.com

Travel To Jersey from the UK

By Air

Direct passenger services to the island are available from the following airlines:

Aurigny Air Services
☎ 01481 822886 (reservations) or ☎ 01534 743568
www.aurigny.com
Departs from: Bristol, East Midlands, Gatwick, Manchester, Southampton, Stansted

Air Southwest
☎ 0870 241 8202 (Reservations)
0870 043 4553 (General Enquiries)
www.airsouthwest.com
Departs from: Bristol, Plymouth

Blue Islands
☎ 08456 202122
www.blueislands.com
Departs from: Southampton

BMI Baby
☎ 09058 282828
www.bmibaby.com
Departs from: Birmingham, Manchester,
East Midlands, Cardiff

British Airways
☎ 0844 4930787 (UK)
www.britishairways.com

Departs from: London Gatwick

Cityjet
☎ 0871 666 50 50
www.cityjet.com
Departs from: London City

Flybe
☎ 0871 700 2000/01392 268529
www.flybe.com
Departs from: Birmingham, Bristol, Exeter, Gatwick, Manchester, Southampton

Manx2
☎ 0871 200 0440
www.manx2.com
Departs from: Gloucester, Isle of Man

Travel From Jersey

By Air

To Paris (Charles de Gaulle)

Flybe
☎ 0871 700 2000/01392 268529
www.flybe.com

To Dinard

Aurigny Air Services
☎ 01481 822886 (reservations) or ☎ 01534 743568
www.aurigny.com

To Guernsey

Aurigny Air Services
☎ 01481 822886 (reservations) or ☎ 01534 743568
www.aurigny.com

Blue Islands
☎ 08456 202122
www.blueislands.com

Flybe
☎ 0871 700 2000/01392 268529
www.flybe.com

To Alderney

Aurigny Air Services
☎ 01481 822886 (reservations) or
☎ 01534 743568
www.aurigny.com

By Sea
Condor
☎ 01202 207216
www.condorferries.co.uk
Elizabeth Terminal,
St Helier Harbour
Departures to: St Malo, Guernsey, Poole, Weymouth (Fast Ferry) and Portsmouth (conventional ferry) – Drive On Drive Off.

Manche Îles Express
☎ 01534 880756
Albert Quay, St Helier
Departures to: The other Channel Islands and three ports in Normandy (no cars).

Day Excursions to France
A valid passport is essential for even a day trip to France.

National Trust

All National Trust members are admitted free to National Trust of Jersey sites. However some are private homes. Contact their HQ ☎ 01534 483193 for further details of what access may be available.
www.nationaltrustjersey.org.je

Sports

Cricket
Matches played at the FB Playing Fields, Grève d'Azette; Victoria College Grounds or at Grainville, St Saviour's Hill, St Saviour Sports Ground.

Croquet
Jersey Croquet Club
Les Quennervais Sports Centre
St Brelade
☎ 01534 499932
www.mnlg.com/jcc

Fishing
Coarse Fishing
There are two day-ticket waters on the island: Millbrook and Dannemarche

reservoirs. More information is available from the Jersey Freshwater Angling Association.

☎ 01534 701162/861083

Freshwater Angling

For rudd, roach, perch, carp, bream, tench, chubb, eels and trout. Maggots not allowed in reservoirs.

Sea Angling

All year round, fish of all varieties from places such as Bouley Bay, Bonne Nuit, Rozel and St Catherine's breakwater where rods and reels can be hired, plus bait at the kiosk on the breakwater. These spots are in the north of the island.

On the south coast, St Helier town harbour, Elizabeth Castle breakwater, St Aubin's harbour and St Brelade's jetty all produce some good fish. For beach fishing, try St Ouen's Bay, St Aubin's Bay, and Grouville Bay for bass.

The island has a number of sea angling clubs who organize shore and boat festivals in the summer. Tackle shops have details of boat trips which show excellent catches including British records.

As Jersey has some of the highest tides in the world, before fishing from rocks ask local anglers if it is safe to do so.

Trout Fishing

(Fly only). Covers Queen's Valley and Val de la Mare Reservoir, St Ouen. Permits from **Fish Market Tackle Shop,** 7 Beresford Market, St Helier. ☎ 01534 874875

Trout Fly Fishing

Queen's Valley and Val de la Mare. No coarse fishing on either.
No bait on either.

Permits, tackle and bait, for fly, sea and coarse fishing, available from **JFS Sport**, 4 Clos des Pas, Green Street, St Helier. ☎ 01534 758195.

Fitness and Sports Grounds

Fitness First

Waterfront, St Helier
☎ 01534 752400/0844 571 2883
Open: Mon–Thur 6am–10pm,
Fri 6am–8pm, Sat 7am-8pm,
Sun 8am–6pm.

Fort Regent

St Helier (leisure centre)
☎ 01534 500200
Gym, badminton, squash, table tennis, snooker, bowls. Access via Fort Regent multi-storey car park, Pier Road.

Open: Mon–Thu 6.30am–9.30pm,
Sat & Sun 8.15am–5pm

Jersey Recreation Grounds
Grève d'Azette, St Clement
☎ 01534 721938
Golf, mini-golf, bowls, tennis

Les Ormes
St Brelade
☎ 01534 497000
www.lesormes.je
Golf, gym, tennis, swimming and nw Soccer Dome

Les Quennevais Sports Centre
St Brelade
☎ 01534 490909
Open: (pool) Mon–Fri 7am–8pm,
Sat 9am–5pm, Sun 9am–7pm.
(gym) Mon–Fri 7am–9pm, Sat and Sun 9am–9pm

Flying
Jersey Aero Club
St Peter
☎ 01534 743990
www.jerseyaeroclub.com
For flying lessons (trial flying lessons).

Golf
La Moye Golf Club
St Brelade
☎ 01534 743401
www.lamoyegolfclub.co.uk
18-hole course, driving range, putting green, golf shop clubhouse and restaurant. Open to visitors who are members of a recognised club – proof of handicap required.

Royal Jersey Golf Club
Grouville
☎ 01534 854416
www.royaljersey.com
18-hole course, putting green, golf shop, clubhouse and
restaurant. Open to visitors who are members of a recognised club proof of handicap required.

Les Ormes Golf & Leisure Club
Mont à la Brune, St Brelade
☎ 01534 497000
www.lesormes.je
9-hole course, 17-bay covered driving range, practice area, golf shop, indoor tennis courts, fitness centre, hair and beauty salon, crêche, bar and restaurant.

Les Mielles Golf & Country Club
Five Mile Road, St Peter
☎ 01534 482787
www.lesmielles.com
18-hole course, driving range, practice area, 18-hole mini-golf, golf shop, laser clay pigeon shoot, bar and restaurant. Open: daily throughout the year from dawn to dusk. Tuition and equipment to buy and hire. Clubs hired.

Jersey Recreation Grounds
Grève d'Azette, St Clement
☎ 01534 721938
9-hole course, putting green, bowls, tennis and restaurant. Open: 9am all year, closes at 3.30–4pm winter and 8.30pm Mon–Fri in season with earlier closing 6.30–7pm Fri–Sat in season. (No clubs hired.)

Wheatlands Golf Course
Les Grupieaux, St Peter
☎ 01534 888844
www.wheatlandsjeresey.com
9-hole course, putting green, bar and garden terrace.

Mini Golf
Jersey Adventure Golf at the Living Legend
La Rue du Petit Aleval, St Peter
☎ 01534 485496

Les Mielles Golf & Country Club
Five Mile Road, St Peter
See above.

Horse Riding
Riding on any beach is prohibited 10.30am-6.00pm May-September.

Bon-Air Stables
La Grande Route de St Laurent, St Lawrence
☎ 01534 865196

Le Claire Riding Stables
Sunnydale, Rue Militaire,
St John
☎ 01534 862823

Sorrel Stables & Saddlery Centre
(livery, saddlery and riding wear)
Mont Fallu, St Peter
☎ 07797 742009
Open daily 9am–5.30pm.
Shop not open on Sunday.

Shooting
Crabbé Clay Pigeon Club
Gréve de Lecq
St Mary.
☎ 01534 876588
Restricted hours apply, telephone for information.

Ten Pin Bowling
Jersey Bowl
Airport Road
St Peter
☎ 01534 490444
18 lanes, pool hall, Quasar, play areas and family restaurant & diner. Open: daily
12am–midnight

Tennis
Caesarean Tennis Club
Grands Vaux
☎ 01534 519177
Courts available to visitors weekdays 9am–6pm; pay court fees to the steward
before play starts.
Professional coach available all year. Only recognised tennis clothing to be
worn.

Les Ormes
St Brelade
☎ 01534 497000
www.lesormes.je
8 indoor bookable courts.

Jersey Recreation Grounds
Grève d'Azette
St Clement
☎ 01534 721938
Rackets and balls for hire.

Water Activities
Cruising and Yachting

The Elizabeth Marina
St Helier
☎ 01534 885530
564 berths.

The Royal Channel Islands Yacht Club
St Aubin
☎ 01534 741023
www.rciyc.je
Visiting yachtsmen are welcome.

The St Helier Yacht Club
South Pier, St Helier
☎ 01534 721307
www.sthelieryachtclub.com
Visiting yachtsmen are welcome.

JerseySailing
New North Quay, St Helier Marina, St Helier
☎ 01534 747738
www.jerseysailing.com
Practical courses and charter facilities available.

South Coast Cruises Ltd
Albert Quay, St Helier
☎ 01534 732466
www.jerseycruises.com
Cruise Jersey's beautiful and historic south coast, up to two trips daily Monday to Saturday. Book at the kiosk near to the town marina. Wheelchairs accepted.

Scuba Diving
Bouley Bay Dive Centre
Bouley Bay
☎ 01534 866990
www.scubadivingjersey.com
5 star PADI facilities, TDI and FreeDiving courses. Regular trips to wrecks around the Channel Islands.

Dive Jersey
H2O Sports, Belmont Road, St Helier
☎ 01534 880934
www.divejersey.co.uk
Diving and dive tuition available all year round. PADI 5 star facilities.

Surfing

St Ouen's Bay is the main break, others include Grève de Lecq, Plémont and St Brelade's Bay. Note you cannot surf between 10am and 6pm from April to October at St Brelade's Bay. Surfing school and hire facilities at:

Laneez School of Surfing
Le Port, St Ouen's Bay
☎ 01534 744157
www.surfjersey.je
All courses provided by fully qualified instructors. Boards and wetsuit hire.

Jersey Surf School
Surf Shak,
St Ouen's Bay (seasonal)
☎ 01534 484005
www.jerseysurfschool.co.uk
Surf lessons, board and wetsuit hire. BSA approved.

Seasport Centres

Active Island Sports
Wayside Slip, St Brelade's Bay (seasonal)
☎ 07797 717564
www.activeislandsports.com
Windsurfing, sailing and canoeing. Equipment provided.

Jersey Sea Sport Centre
La Haule Slip, St Aubin
(seasonal)
☎ 07797 738180
www.jerseyseasport.com
Jet skis, speed boat trips, banana rides, wakeboarding and water-skiing. Equipment and tuition provided.

Surf & Sun Watersports
St Brelade's Bay
☎ 07797 736411
www.surfandsun.co.uk
Waterskiing, wakeboarding, canoes. Wetsuits provided.

Pure Adventure Ltd
☎ 01534 769165
www.purejersey.com

Gorey Watersports Centre
St Brelade's Bay
☎ 07797 816258
www.goreywatersports.com
Waterskiing, wakeboarding, speed boats, banana rides and sea kayaks. Equipment and tuition provided

Swimming
Aqua Splash
The Waterfront, St Helier
☎ 01534 734524
Open: Mon–Fri 7am–10pm,
Sat and Sun 8am–8pm.
25-metre pool, leisure pool, wave machine, flume/tyre-ride, sauna.

Havres des Pas Swimming Pool
St Helier
No charge.
☎ 01534 728782
Open: may to Sept. lifeguards on duty 10am–6pm. Seawater pool dating from 1895

Les Quennevais Sports Centre
St Brelade
☎ 01534 490909
Open: Mon–Fri 7am–8pm, Sat 9am–5pm, Sun 9am–7pm.

Useful addresses, telephone numbers & websites

Jersey Heritage
Jersey Museum
Weighbridge, St Helier
☎ 01534 633300
www.jerseyheritage.org
Queries about museums, historic sites etc.

States of Jersey
Tourist Information Centre
Liberation Square, St Helier
☎ 01534 448800
Fax 01534 448898
Open: Mon–Fri 8.30am–5.30pm, Sat & Sun 9am-1pm; closed on Sunday Oct to Dec.

Telephone Numbers

Customs & Immigration

☎ 01534 448000

Directory Enquires ☎ 1185384

Flight Enquiries ☎ 01534 446000

Fire, Police, Ambulance, Sea Rescue ☎ 999

Hospital ☎ 01534 442000 (see also p.184)

Jersey area code ☎ 01534 from UK (+44 1534 from other countries)

Harbourmaster ☎ 01534 447788

Weather Shipping ☎ 09006 690022

Tourist Information ☎ 01534 448800

Mobile telephones

Please note that mobile telephones will need an international roaming facility to work in Jersey, and that some pay as you go networks do not operate on the island. Please check with your telephone provider before travelling.

Websites

www.jersey.com

www.jerseytravel.com

www.thisisjersey.com

www.tripadvisor.com

Useful Information

Banks

Hours of business are usually 9.30am–4.30pm daily. Some banks open Saturday 9.30am–12.30pm. Most major credit cards and Euro cards are accepted. There are Link card machines in St Helier, St Peter, Red Houses and St Saviour. Currency not legal tender in UK.

Bureaux de Change

All banks, head post office, Jersey Airport, St Helier and Gorey harbours and several travel agents.

Beach Safety

Before setting off to the water's edge at low tide, it is advisable to check tide times. Always keep an eye on the water flow – the tide comes in surprisingly fast along much of the coast, and it is so easy to be 'cut off' by the tide whilst you are low water fishing for crabs and winkles.

There are several beaches that are notorious for having strong currents. These beaches are often patrolled by lifeguards during the day throughout the summer season. Warning flags are placed along the beach that are colour coded to signify the following sea conditions:

Yellow flag: dangerous conditions.
Red flag: do not enter the water.
Red and yellow flag combined: swimming area patrolled by lifeguards.

It is important to mention that no flag doesn't mean it is safe to go in the water. Check first the weather forecast, tide times, wind conditions and state of the sea.

Camping and Caravanning

All campsites have adequate separate toilet facilities for men and women. Caravans and motorhomes can only be accommodated on the sites listed below. Size restrictions apply and visitors are advised to contact their chosen campsite in advance for details. It is illegal to camp anywhere other than on a recognised and approved campsite.

Beuvelande Camp Site
St Martin
☎ 01534 853575
www.campingjersey.com
Open: 1 May–15 Sept.

Bleu Soleil Camping
Leoville, St Ouen
☎ 01534 481007
www.bleusoleilcamping.com
Open: May–Sep

Rose Farm
St Brelade.
☎ 741231
Open: May–Sept.

Rozel Camping Park
La Grande Route De Rozel,
St Martin
☎ 01534 855200
www.rozelcamping.co.uk
Open:mid-May to mid-Sept

Currency

The island, although using the sterling denominations of pounds and pence, has its own distinctive currency which is only legal tender in the Channel Islands. UK currency is also accepted everywhere in the island.

Disabled Toilets

Disabled toilets have Radar locks. For £5 deposit keys can be borrowed from St Helier Town Hall ☎ 01534 601690.

Duty Free Allowances

Tobacco Goods
200 cigarettes or 100 cigarillos (up to 3 grams each) or 50 cigars or 350 grams of tobacco.

Alcoholic Drinks
1 litre of distilled beverages or spirits OR 4 litres of sparkling or fortified wines and 4 litres of other wines.

Perfume
Perfume 60oo/ml and Toilet Water 250 cc/ml.

Other Goods
Amount £340

Emergency Services

Fire, Police, Ambulance, Sea Rescue ☎ 999 or 112.
'Visitors' Clinics' are available all over the island (see under Medical Treatment').

General Hospital
Gloucester Street
St Helier
☎ 01534 442000
Offers visitors general outpatient, accident and emergency facilities (entrance in The Parade), also a visitors' clinic.

Liberation Day

9 May public holiday, most shops closed.
Thursday of week which includes 15 September: Battle of Britain Air Display at St Aubin's Bay.

Jersey's Flag and Arms

With Jersey having so many of its services to the public administered locally, with distinctively island features, it is not surprising that the island also has its own flag. This is a red saltire on a white background to which has been added the Jersey arms surmounted by the Plantagenet crown. This has flown from island flagstaffs on festive and important occasions, together with the Union Jack, for over 200 years.

Jersey's arms, which often appear on public buildings and smaller items, such as tourist information and coins, are the three royal leopards. They originate from the seal granted to the Bailiwick by Edward I in 1279, a replica of the armorial bearings of every English monarch since Richard I, still to be seen on today's royal standard.

Language

The principal language of Jersey is English, but in view of the island's proximity to France it is no surprise that the influence of that country's language is always evident. Until the nineteenth century, the language spoken on Jersey was Jèrriais, which was derived from Norman French. This language still survives, although at the last census in 2001 it had fewer than 3,000 speakers.

Today, Jersey's official languages are English and French, and a dialect called Jersey Legal French is still used for some official documents. Visitors to the Channel Islands are sometimes surprised at the pronunciation of place names; partly as a result of the anglicisation of the islands, it is usual to hear even French names pronounced in an English rather than a French manner.

Library Service

Books are available to tourists against a returnable deposit.

Jersey Library

Halkett Place, St Helier
☎ 01534 448700, reference section 01534 448701
Open: Mon, Wed–Fri 9.30am–5.30pm;
Tue 9.30am–7.30pm;
Sat 9.30am–4pm.

Les Quennevais Branch Library

St Brelade
☎ 01534 448733
Mon–Fri 2–5.30pm, Sat 9.30am–1pm.

Markets

There are two fresh food markets in St Helier: Halkett Place for meat, fruit, flowers, vegetables; Beresford Street for fish, fruit, flowers and vegetables.

Medical Treatment

The reciprocal health care agreement under which UK residents were eligible for free medical treatment in Jersey expired in 2009. While treatment carried out in Jersey's Accident & Emergency department will still be free of charge, any other medical treatment on the island, including operations, GP consultations or any other health-related services will be liable to a charge. It is therefore strongly recommended that all visitors should arrange adequate medical insurance prior to their visit. One option is the service that has been set up by Jersey Tourism specifically for UK visitors: Jersey Travel Insurance (☎ 0845 260 1527; www. jerseytravelinsurance.com).

Most of the GP surgeries on the island provide a service for holiday visitors, but you should check their scale of charges when making an appointment. An out of hours service is also available through GP surgeries. Prescriptions can be dispensed at any pharmacy; a charge will be payable. Reciprocal healthcare agreements still exist for visitors from Australia, Austria, Barbados, France, Ice-

land, New Zealand, Norway, Portugal and Sweden.
Health and Social Services department:
☎ 01534 445500
www.gov.je/health

Newspapers, Television & Radio

The *Jersey Evening Post* is published every day except Sunday and is on sale from about 3.30pm on weekdays and noon on Saturdays at all newsagents. As well as reporting the local news and giving a summary of national and international news, its other daily features include the weather, times of high and low tides, together with the evening's programme of listening and viewing on radio and television. The Friday and Saturday editions of the *JEP*, as it is known locally, carry the times of the next Sunday's religious services and the Saturday edition has 'The Island Diary' – a synopsis of 'What's On' for the following week.www.thisisjersey.com

Channel Television is the smallest station in the Independent Broadcasting Authority's network and has four local news and weather reports: at 9.50am, (after ITN News). It also relays local features from time to time. Channel Television is located on the ITV waveband and starts broadcasting at 6am, carrying on throughout the day. www.channeltv.co.uk

BBC Radio Jersey has the highest listener population ratio of any of the local radio stations. It broadcasts on VHF 88.8 MHz and 1026 kHz (292m)and on DAB. 'What's On' bulletins are broadcast daily between 7am and 9am. Channel 103 (103.7MHz) is Jersey'sindependent local radio station.

Passports

Citizens of Great Britain and of the Irish Republic do not require passports to enter Jersey. A passport is essential to visit France, even on a day trip. All airline passengers require photo ID.

Post Offices

Main post office for counter services, Bureau de Change, Intelpost, Datapost, National Savings, Girobank and enquiries is situated in Broad Street, St Helier ☎ 01534 616616; Open: weekdays 8.30am-5pm, (opens at 9am on Wed).

Jersey has also been issuing its own postage stamps since 1969 and these are much admired and widely collected by philatelists. The commemoratives have portrayed famous Jersey personalities such as actress Lillie Langtry, artist Edmund Blampied and golfer Harry Vardon. It should be noted that JERSEY STAMPS MUST BE USED ON ALL OUTGOING MAIL.

Radio

BBC Radio Jersey
18, Parade Road, St Helier
☎ 01534 870000
radiojersey@bbc.co.uk
(VHF 88.8MHz and 1026kHz [292m])

Channel 103 FM
6 Tunnell Street,
St Helier.
☎ 01534 888103
www.channel103.com
(103.7MHz FM)

Self-catering Holidays
Freedom Holidays
40 New Street
St Helier
☎ 01534 725259
www.freedomholidays.com

Macole's Holidays
☎ 01534 488100
www.macoles.com

Speedboats, Surfboards and Sailboards
Must be registered at St Helier Harbour Office as soon as possible on arrival.
☎ 01534 447788

Shopping
Shopping on holiday never seems to be the rushed chore it is back home and this is particularly true for visitors to Jersey. St Helier has a fine shopping area as well as quaint back streets where there is a wide range of goods and services — all VAT free. Jewellery and perfume are especially good buys and there are plenty of places to get those holiday snaps printed. There are also the covered Central Market in Halkett Place and the Fish Market in Beresford Street to wander round. The flowers, the umbrellas of the cafés, the benches set out at regular intervals, all give St Helier a leisured, continental air and make it a pleasurable centre for shopping.

Index

Published by:
Horizon Editions Ltd (trading as Horizon Press)
The Oaks,Moorfarm Rd., Ashbourne,Derbyshire, UK
email: stella@thehorizonpress.co.uk

9th edition 2010
ISBN 13: 978-1-84306-450-3

British Library Cataloguing in Publication Data: a catalogue record for this book is
available from the British Libary.

Print: Gomer Press, Llandysul, Ceredigion, Wales

Design: Mark Titterton

Editor: Ian Howe

Front cover: Portelet Bay on the South West Coast. (Jersey Tourism)

Back cover top: Firing the midday gun at Elizabeth Castle.

Back cover bottom: Battle of the Flowers. (Jersey Tourism)

Acknowledgements
The author would like to thank the following for help with the preparation of this book:
the Constables of the twelve parishes, the Town Greffier, Mr P. Freely, Mr Mike Tait of Jersey Tourism, Centenier A. Vibert, Miss Jean Arthur, Mr R. W. Le Sueur, Mr Leslie Sinel, Mrs K. Paget-Tomlinson, Mrs Rosemary Hampton, Mr L. Hamon of Jersey Motor Transport,
Miss Cienne Jurd, Mr A Crosby and Mr M. K. Doong.
The Publisher would also like to thank the following: Jersey Tourism,
Jersey Heritage Trust and The National Trust Jersey.

Photography
Jersey Tourism: Front cover; Back cover bottom; p.10; p.15 both; p.18; p.23; p.31 both; p.35;
p.38; p.39 all; p.47 bottom; p.62; p.63 bottom; p.74; p.78; p.87 bottom; p.90; p.91; p102; p.106
p.115 both; p.118 all; p.123 both; p.131 top; p.138; p.139; p.142; 154 (right); p.155; p.158.
National Trust Jersey: p.130 (top); p.159
La Mare Vineyard: p.134.
Other photography by Lindsey Porter.